HEART & SOUL

by
Hayward Nishioka

This book is recommended by:

UNITED STATES JUDO, INC.

UNITED STATES JUDO FEDERATION

UNITED STATES JUDO ASSOCIATION

OHARA 🗓 **PUBLICATIONS, INCORPORATED**
SANTA CLARITA, CALIFORNIA

DEDICATION

Some talk, and do little.
Some talk little, but do much.
This book is dedicated to
M. Uyehara
The one person who has
done more to advance the
martial arts than any other.

Graphic Concept Design: Joanne Oka Benites
Graphic Design: Blumhoff Design
Proofreaders: Deborah Overman & Sara Fogan

Various photos: Courtesy of Rainbow Publications, Inc.

PREFACE

As I reflect on my experiences in a sport that has so altered my life, I can't help but feel some embarrassment and sadness at the thought that this is an exercise in vanity justification. Some time from now, these words will be forgotten. Do you want to suppose that someone will even remember your book tomorrow?

Still, I must try. There may be someone out there who may find some solace in common thoughts and experiences. The one thing *judoka* (judo practitioners) have been negligent in is celebrating through words the unique and intoxicating experiences obtained through judo training. Hopefully, this book will do a little of that, as well as provide guideposts to direct your path.

We are each special entities whose very existence is no less than awe-inspiring. First of all, in all the universe we can only contemplate that there may be another planet that holds the promises of life as we know it here on Earth.

Imagine there are between twelve to 200 million sperm in one ejaculation. The average couple performs intercourse an average of three times per week. At the low end, that's 144 million sperm a month searching for existence. To complicate matters, each woman provides only one egg per month. You were the chance result of the union of that one egg and the chosen sperm. You get to live out of your domain and to be the best in your selected endeavor. Now, that's a miracle!

Good luck on your journey. May you find these bits of information entertaining as well as informative.

This book has been divided into the following sections: Preparatory, Technical, Strategic and Aftermath. They are self-explanatory. The vignettes in this book are not there to provide answers to your questions. In fact, you may not even find answers to your questions in this book. The purpose of these stories is to spark intuitive thought and discussion.

ABOUT THE AUTHOR

A member of the *Black Belt* Hall of Fame (1968, Judo Competitor of the Year and 1977, Judo Instructor of the Year), Hayward Nishioka is not only one of America's premier *judoka* but is also a black belt in karate. Born in Los Angeles in 1942 of Japanese-American parentage, he began his career in the martial arts at the age of 12 when his father, a judo black belt, dressed him in an impromptu *gi* consisting of an old army jacket and put him through the paces on a hardwood floor.

Soon afterward that same year (1954), Nishioka began training in judo under Ryusei Inouye at Sen Shin Dojo in East Los Angeles, and in 1955 began training in karate under Tsutomu Ohshima. He received his first-degree black belt in judo in 1957 at age 15 from the U.S. Judo Federation while he was still training under Inouye. From 1959 to 1960, Nishioka studied judo with Kenneth Kuniyuki at Seinan Dojo in southwest Los Angeles.

After graduating from Los Angeles Roosevelt High School in 1960 he traveled to Japan to further his study of both judo and karate. He spent 12 months at Tenri University in Nara studying under Yasuichi Matsumoto, who was the champion of the first-ever All-Japan Judo Championships and one of the art's most respected instructors. From Nara, he moved to Tokyo, where he enrolled as a special student at the Kodokan, the noted headquarters of Japanese judo. While at the Kodokan, he was honored along with James Bregman, another noted judoka, as being the first foreigners to demonstrate the *nage-no-kata* at the 1961 All-Japan Judo Championships. Also while at the Kodokan, he studied *shotokan* karate under Shigeru Egami, the direct disciple of Gichin Funakoshi.

Nishioka returned to the United States in 1963. Progressing rapidly in the martial arts, it wasn't long before he began to accumulate an impressive list of accomplishments as a judo and karate competitor. As a judo competitor, he won the coveted Pan-American Games gold medal in 1967; he won the United States AAU National Grand Championship in 1965 and the National Championships in 1965, 1966 and 1970; he placed fourth in the 1967 World Judo Championships; and he has been National Masters Champion in the 189-pound division many times. Twice overall champion in kata 1978, 79 with teammate Jim Yamashita and member of four United States International teams.

As a karate competitor, he won the 1965 Nisei Week Karate Championships. As of the 2000s, Nishioka is a 7th-degree black belt in judo and a *shodan* (first-degree black belt) in karate. (Nishioka has twice been inducted into the *Black Belt* Hall of Fame: as the first Judo Competitor of the Year in 1968; and as Judo Instructor of theYear in 1978.)

In 1968, he acquired an associate's degree from Los Angeles City College. He later acquired a bachelor's degree (1972) and master's degree (1974) in physical education, and a master's degree (1975) in administrative education from California State College, Los Angeles. Soon afterward (1975), he became an assistant professor of physical education at Los Angeles City College, where he has instituted one of the more extensive martial arts programs in the United States. He became a full professor of physical education in 1980, and as of 2000 still continues to teach there.

Nishioka has done much to promote the growth of judo. He is the founder and first president of the Southern California Collegiate Judo Conference (1977-1980). He has been a member of the Board of Directors of the Southern California Judo Association (NANKA) since 1968, a life member of the United States Judo Association (1978), the United States Judo Federation (1977) and United States Judo Inc. (the national governing body of judo in the United States) in 1984. He was the president of California Judo Inc. (1980-1983) and an athletes' representative to United States Judo Inc. (1980-1984). Nishioka has served on several committees for U.S. Judo Inc. and the U.S. Judo Federation. He has also been a class "A" national coach since 1980 and a class "A" International Judo Federation referee since 1991. In 1978, the National Collegiate Judo Association voted him Coach of the Year. Nishioka was technical advisor at the 1996 summer Olympics in Atlanta, Georgia.

Drawing from his considerable knowledge of all aspects of the martial arts, he has written several articles on the subject for *Black Belt* and *Karate/Kung Fu Illustrated* magazines as well as the book *The Judo Textbook*, and *Foot Throws* published by Ohara Publications, Inc. He has also conducted many forums, clinics and training sessions. He also produced and directed over 50 Judo videos and is a member of S.A.G. (Screen Actors Guild)

All his achievements and successes in the martial arts notwithstanding, Nishioka's most important and proudest accomplishment of all is his three wonderful children: Faith, Alicia and Eric.

FOREWORD

Judo... *Judo.* Any writing on my father should begin and end with this word. The space between which would contain forty-four years, and not one day passed between them which were empty of thoughts of judo. What follows this page are some of the many observations my father has made and taken away from judo, but what goes unsaid is a small collection of his personal memories which I will now try and briefly unpack. They begin, as all judoka know, with a picture of Kano sitting, watching his idea move *alive.* We thank him more in our *uki goshi* than we ever did with a bow. Next, the smell of a dojo; Cornhusks? No, better. There in no other like it. The faded green ribbon of a medal from the Pan American Games, stubbed toes from old canvas mats, the heater and makeshift shower room with its tilted floor at Seinan dojo, trophies—actual. metal ones—with small figurines frozen in *seionage— uchimata—osoto-gari,* two piles: one of *zoris* and one of *gis* heaped on a judoka for warmth during a particularly cold winter, and finally a snapshot of Ushijima, "calves thick as thighs, small, balding and tough as nails."

Prior to judo, which unfolds to me through photographs and pieced together stories, is my father growing up in East Los Angeles in the late 1940s. He stares out from these photographs—impossibly young. For awhile, my grandmother was the sole support for a family of three. When she finally remarried, she unknowingly found a life and love for her son also, for she had married a judoka. My grandfather is where my father really starts and it is important that his name, Dan Oka, should help begin this book, simply because his understanding of a twelve-year-old boy's need for something of his own, inspired the love which wrote it. I cannot over emphasize the impact my grandfather has had on my father's life. He took him to his first tournament. It was a long time ago, far enough back that instead of medals, winners left with sake, shoyu and hundred pound sacks of rice. It was here, at Nishi Hongangi Temple that my father first really *saw* judo. He watched wide-eyed as they cleared the mat for the black belts who entered and filed down the center aisle to take their seats mat-side. For at least one young boy they were giants, and the temple—over-filled—pressed to contain the force of their size. My father could not forget what he could not express until at home, on a wooden floor, in old army jackets, my grandfather, threw him over and over again. My father, continually bruising his heels loved every moment, loved his father, loved judo.

Once I saw my father doing a spinning *uchimata*. I had never seen one before. No one else was watching, but I knew that if all of his work had converged at that point, unnoticed, under dingy lighting, he was still able to make a promise—small, delicate, terribly important—of joy. That throw, father, it sings for me still. *Judo.*

Alicia Nishioka

Contents

CHAPTER 1
PREPARATORY

CHAPTER 2
TECHNICAL

CHAPTER 3
STRATEGIC

CHAPTER 4
AFTERMATH

CHAPTER 1

PREPARATORY

"JUMBI"

ジュンビ

U.S. Senator and *judoka* Ben "Nighthorse" Campbell with Hayward Nishioka at the Olympic Training Center.

JUDO: THE MULTI-FACETED SPORT 1.1

It's an Olympic sport. It's an art form. It's a character-builder. It's cultural. It's self-defense. It's aerobic. It's anaerobic. It's healthy. It's technical. It's spiritual. It's recreational. It's philosophical. It's mental. It's physical. It's a fraternity. It's a microcosm of life.

During a conversation, my friend Ben Campbell once said this of judo: "Once you've done it you will never forget it. It becomes a part of how you react to life."

Ben is one of the many fine individuals I have had the pleasure of knowing and admiring. A past national judo champion and Olympian; an 8th-degree black belt; a master Indian jeweler, Indian chief, rancher and quarter-horse breeder; a U.S. Congressman and, in 1996, U.S. Senator from Colorado, Ben Campbell is a fine role model for young *judoka* (judo practitioners) to follow.

Miracles exist all around us. They're simply fantasies that have taken form from the minds of individuals like you and I. If in the 1890s someone had predicted that we would be able to talk instantly to someone on the other side of the world, see copies of miniature people in a small box, moving about or speaking, or travel across countries or oceans at speeds of over 500 miles per hour, they would not have been taken seriously.

All these things exist here in our future. What is now tangible was first intangible. They were once dreams, fantasies and thoughts created by the wonderful and powerful instrument known as the mind. If we put our minds to it, everything is possible. Even the most outrageous is possible, given the right circumstances. What about this for a dream? You're in your mid-30s, you're racked with injuries, and you're plagued with financial problems and a declining love life. However, you're competing in the Olympic games, and you made it into the finals. Your opponent looks like Arnold Schwarzenegger, and he's wearing an illegal, undersized judo *gi* (uniform). The guy is all muscle, with a scowl on his face and pimples popping off his cheek muscles. You bow, grasp hold of King Kong, and what's the outcome? Think!

If you defeated him easily, it wasn't impossible to defeat him after all. If you fought a difficult match but you won, you worked hard and therefore deserved to win. If you lost, you didn't have a prayer in the first place. This brings a thought to my mind. If we don't have dreams, how are we going to make them come true?

Photo by Christine Penick Lincoln

Your body can possibly do whatever you want it to do. All you need is an idea of what you want to do. It's the thought that counts!

Practice your throw over and over during *randori* training, then attend a
tournament and spar with an opponent. If the opportunity to use the
throw avails itself, the throw will happen out of nowhere. That's *waza*.

SEE IT AS IT IS   1.3

Some *judoka* try to offset their opponent's superior skills with something other than their own skill. They'll try for more power, more aerobic conditioning, more strategy, more willpower. Why not try raising skill level?

Strength, aerobic conditioning, strategy, skill and willpower are all important components of the package used to gain success. Of these components, what makes judo unique is the component of technique. But honing one's skill level requires more time and energy than just strength, aerobic capacity or willpower.

This is not to discount the importance of the other components of the success package. It's just that when you come down to it, judo is technique-oriented first. If it were not so, a weightlifter or a long-distance runner would be world champion in judo. Judo anyone?

"Man, I was breathing so hard and my whole body felt weak and tired. My mouth was dry, and my throat and chest were sore. I couldn't help it; he just came in from nowhere and I went flying." Sound familiar?

The operative word here is "shape." You've got to be "in shape" if you're going to compete. But what is "shape," and how do you know if you're "in shape"? Basically, but not always, if you can finish your match, begin your next match immediately afterward and go the distance, you're probably in shape.

To compete at the elite level, additional training is a necessity. One type of training is aerobic (cardiovascular) conditioning, and the other type of training is anaerobic (endurance and power) conditioning. Here, I'm talking about endurance training for judo competitors.

To gain endurance, a rule of thumb is to exercise at a steady pace for 20 to 25 minutes four times a week. It's also wise to vary your routine; don't do the same routine every day. Exercises could include running, swimming, aerobics or cycling. The recommended way to test whether you are exercising strenuously enough is to monitor your heart rate. On the safe side, your heart rate is 220 beats per minute minus your age. To calculate the heart rate for a 22-year-old, for example, subtract 22 from the maximum heart rate of 220 beats per minute, and then multiply the remainder by point seven ($(220-22) \times .7$). This equates to 138.6 beats per minute. Therefore, as a 22-year-old is running or exercising, his heart should beat 138.6 times per minute.

Once your body becomes acclimated to this pace, you can increase the intensity level of your workout to meet your requirements. After a while, you will know what your body can sustain and will know how to adjust yourself to the exercise without stopping to measure your heart rate all the time. Just be sensitive to how your body reacts to the workout. You will know when you're in too much pain or when you're ready to step up to the next level. The heart rate of highly conditioned athletes in training is between 180 to 190 beats per minute. And that's at about 80 percent of their maximum effort. Some Olympic athletes train at 90 percent of their maximum effort.

It's no fun when you're gasping for air rather than looking for an opportunity to defeat your opponent. When you're in shape, you are more capable of attacking more times per minute without getting tired and making mistakes. Once you begin an endurance training program, it will take at least six weeks before you feel any difference in your body's newfound ability to process oxygen.

Photo by Hayward Nishioka

National Collegiate Judo Champion Ramon Rivera is shown training in high altitude at Big Bear, California.

Photo © Bob Willingham, 1998

Sixteen-year-old Sun Kye of North Korea made history at the 1996 Olympics when, without doubt or hesitation, she defeated Ryoko Tamura of Japan to win the first gold medal anyone from her country ever won in any Olympic sport. She also became the youngest person ever to win an Olympic gold medal in judo, dispelling the myth that it takes years to become an Olympic champion.

TO CHAMPION OR NOT TO CHAMPION 1.5

Some people are afraid to be in first place. That's right. Let me say it again. Some people are afraid to be in first place. It's always nice to be the hopeful and the up-and-coming competitor. It's no fun to be the one who has arrived and will soon be a "has-been."

Let me say this. "Has-beens" will never be "wanna-bes" and "never-weres." Champions will always be champions. Champions will always know what it was like to be a champion and, more importantly, will know how to become one again.

When they are faced with a choice to compete for the top spot, champions without hesitation will opt to go for the gold. Those who have never been in that position sometimes wonder if they belong there. However, this doubt in themselves and in their ability is an added invisible opponent. You don't need to fight more than one opponent at a time. The outcome will be more positive if you resign yourself to doing your best. Never mind whether you belong there or that your opponent is bigger, stronger or uglier. Just go for it! Tread on ground you've never tread before. Be a champion.

"Gambare" is a Japanese word that means "tough it out!" or "be tough!"

During the 1984 Olympics a gymnast from Japan with a broken leg mounted the rings in pain, completed his routine and dismounted from about seven and one-half feet, landing on both legs. Yasuhiro Yamashita, in the final match against Mohammed Rashwan of Egypt, fought with an injured knee and could barely walk. Arthur Shnabel of the Federal Republic of Germany, even though he was 38 years old and was probably older than the other fighters, won a berth on the Olympic team and won a bronze medal in the open weight division. Joe Walters, a disabled Vietnam veteran, was Masters Champion several times. He has one leg.

I have no doubt that someone at one time or another told them to tough it out, and they did. "Gambare!"

Yasuhiro Yamashita had been the all-Japan champion nine times and the world champion twice, but he missed the 1980 Olympic Games due to the U.S. lead boycott which Japan also supported. He was about to miss his chance at an Olympic title in 1984 due to an injury, but something inside him said "Gambare!"

When thinking of failed potential, you need only think of some of your past rivals who had all the tools, e.g., strength, quickness, toughness, technique, aerobic capacity, etc., but somehow didn't make it. You could see that they had a lot of possibilities but instead they drifted away. They probably couldn't see what they had.

Reverend Robert Schuller, in a sermon, once told a story that both illustrates the importance of your environment and causes some sadness in an unfulfilled existence that should have been better. It's a story about an eagle egg that fell out of a tree. A farmer out hiking found the egg and placed it in a chicken's nest, where it hatched. The baby eagle followed his adopted brothers and sisters, pecking for food and hopping around like a chicken all day.

One day, he looked up and saw an eagle flying high above him. Oh, how beautiful it seemed with its soaring wings

Photo courtesy of Hayward Nishioka

Hayward Nishioka is standing in the Tenri University *Dojo* with champions Mickey Tsuchida (left) and U.S. coach Haruo Imamura (center). Many judo champions trained at the Tenri dojo, and they continue to do so.

Illustration by Hayward Nishioka

It's an eagle's lair.

spread wide among the clouds. "If only I could fly like that!" he thought.

The days passed and the eagle eventually died, never knowing he was an eagle or that he could soar high above the Earth. Well, when you hang out with chickens, you'll be a chicken. When you hang out with eagles, you'll fly.

Although it is fictional, this story illustrates the effect that your environment has on your potential for success. While your possibilities may be great, unless you're in the right place at the right time, you're limited by your surroundings. So stay around winners. Stay around people who care. Stay around people who can give you positive critiques and can benefit your progress. Build a support system of friends and competitors. Stay around winners. Be a winner.

Have you ever watched a dance performance or heard a singer so compelling, beautiful, etc. that it made the hair on the back of your neck stand up? Some performances raise the human soul to higher levels of existence. If you have ever felt this before, as tears flowed from your eyes from the mixed emotions churning inside you due to the performance you just witnessed, you know excellence is there for the taking.

Judo matches can also be moving. As you witness some judo bouts, you know there is electricity on the mat. Will against will is exemplified in movements that raise these matches high above the rest. One such match was the final of the 1987 World Championships, in which Yuri Sokolov of the Soviet Union fought Yosuke Yamamoto of Japan. Each fighter escalated the score, and the advantage see-sawed back and forth, until finally time ran out and Yamamoto won. Had there been another minute left on the clock, Sokolov may have been World Champion instead. Both attacked without hesitation, whether ahead or behind. The only thing that mattered was that they fulfill their destiny within that short, decisive, five-minute match.

It was one of those matches in which everyone in the stadium grew silent and focused on the mat as if they were hypnotized. For everyone instinctively knew that they would not witness a match like this ever again. The willpower, strength, skill, speed, tempo and electricity of this particular match would be but a memory in five minutes. It was inspirational.

It is important that you remember those magical moments because they will never happen exactly the same way again. Hopefully they will spur you on in your own quest for excellence.

Photo by Hayward Nishioka

1984 Olympic bronze medalist Ed Liddie pops in with a *seoinage* to upend his stubborn opponent. As of 1998, Liddie is the head judo coach at the Olympic Training Center in Colorado Springs, Colorado.

Yuko Emoto continues to stretch her leg skyward in a Herculean effort to pull Belgium's Gella Vandecaveye onto her back to win the match and the judo gold medal at the 1996 Olympics in Atlanta, Georgia.

"ISHO KEMEI"

Can a person practice a lie? Can a person be deceptive in a workout? When is a person honest in a workout? Whatever their motives are, people can be dishonest during a practice session. For example, you don't want your opponent to know what your favorite technique feels like. In fact, you want him to think your best throw is an *osotogari* (outside major reap) when in fact it is a drop *ippon seoinage* (one- or two-armed shoulder throw dropping to the floor). So what do you do? Attack with the osotogari and not utilize the seoinage at all.

In an honest workout, you want to do the very best that you can. You attack with your favorite throw using everything you've got. This is usually the best way to work out. You want to put your whole being into your workout. You want to lose yourself in your workout session. Thoughts of mundane problems and worries about the workplace or personal relations are forgotten for the moment in favor of honing your skills with your opponent, regardless of whether you may give away an advantage or find that he may be better.

In a true workout, thoughts of strategy, ill will or good will take a backseat to the effort of being pure and honest in your movement. In a word, this is a quest for self, which in Japanese is *"isho kemei."* Isho kemei means "for life" or "for one's dear life." It means to practice as if your life depended not on the outcome, but on your wholehearted effort to transform your judo.

Sibili si ergo
Fortebusis inero
Nobili deis trux
Siuatis inim
Cousin dux

The crux of this saying is that we should not look at
something in a glorified way and miss what it really is.
This is the English translation:

See Billy see her go
Forty buses in a row
No Billy them is trucks
See what's in them
Cows and ducks.

Westerners like to look to the East and read more into it
than what is there. I'm constantly told that judo is a great
spiritual and mental discipline, which it might well be.
Nonetheless, what we learn and become is due to our
interaction with the environment and others around us.

Without our body, we can't learn and nourish the mind
with experiences that elevate the soul. Therefore, primary
and essential to progress in judo is the development of
the body.

Therefore, if we try to separate the relationship between
our spirit/mind and our seemingly mundane body, we
lose sight of what we are: human beings subject to the
laws of nature. We have to train our bodies to perform
how we want them to perform. Alas, there seems to be
no secret incantations or formulas, or super pills, to make
us superheroes.

"There is no secret formula from the East, only hard work!"—Doug Rogers, 1964 Olympic silver medalist in judo.

Photo courtesy of Doug Rogers

Doug Rogers, 1964 Olympic silver medalist in judo.

If you want to become skilled at something, you need to desire that skill and practice hard. If you want to become tough, you need to practice against tough opponents. Although skillfulness and toughness may correlate somewhat, they are attained in different ways.

To attain skillfulness, you need to set up neurological patterns of successful movement. In other words, you have to train your body to do what you want it to do (to perform a certain movement). In judo, this is done by first viewing how a technique is executed, then trying to emulate it by performing *uchikomis* (entry drills) without resistance. The next step is to go through the full range of motion and execute the technique fully. This is accomplished through a practice called *nagekomi*, or sometimes *sutegeiko*, in which the technique is repeatedly executed without resistance.

These repeated executions form neurological pathways. Once your mind has established these patterns, you can practice the new skill under *randori* or free-sparring conditions. This, of course, is a different type of practice since your opponent may now resist or attack at will. What is important in the development of a technique is the ability to execute the technique despite resistance. Therefore, you should select opponents whom you can easily throw. As you become more proficient, you should select tougher and tougher opponents.

In contrast to skill, toughness is developed by practicing with tough opponents who can handle you easily and are less than kind to you.

While repeated practice can develop your skill, you usually don't get a chance to practice your technique when you're sparring with a tough opponent. Usually you're too busy blocking your opponent's attack. In doing so, however, you build a tolerance for his offenses.

In effect, you learn to take a beating and eventually develop your muscles to contract and resist your opponent's techniques. As you become physically successful, you become psychologically aware of the fact that you can take your opponent's punishment; therefore, you become tougher.

If you want skillfulness, work with weaker opponents. If you want toughness, work with the tough.

World and Olympic judo champion Wilhelm Ruska of Holland (throwing his opponent) had both toughness and skill, and he worked hard to achieve these qualities.

Photo courtesy of Hayward Nishioka

Hayward Nishioka is pictured teaching a class at Los Angeles City College. This is his formula for success: determine the goal, make a plan, execute the plan, evaluate the outcome, redo the plan, execute it again, then repeat this again and again.

MAKING YOUR PRACTICE COUNT

Practice sessions can become stale without innovation. If we aimlessly practice without a specific goal in mind and are for a time unsuccessful, we can become bored with our training. We sometimes refer to this time as a "slump." To avoid these slumps, or at least ease them, set small, attainable goals and keep a journal. Here are the steps:

1. Determine your goal, and write it down in your journal.

2. Execute the action toward attaining your goal.

3. Review the results of your actions, and write them down in your journal.

4. Study the previous results to find ways to improve your performance.

5. Re-execute your attempt with the new recommendations for improvement.

6. Study the new results to see if there was a change in your performance.

7. Don't be discouraged if results come slowly.

Sometimes it's nice to just work out without having to plan every move or think about every eventuality. Sometimes it's fun to just immerse yourself in a practice session. But when time is of the essence and you need to prepare for a major tournament, a well-planned schedule for success is difficult to defeat.

(sample)
Judo Diary

Goal:

To throw Yasuhiro Yamashita in practice

Plan:

Practice with him. Look for weaknesses.

Result:

Practice with him indicates weakness to back side.

Problem:

I don't have a throw to back side.

What to do:

1. Practice *kouchigari* left side with others.

2. Practice *seoi* to *kouchi* with others.

Result:

Been practicing two months now. Can feel fairly
confident at throwing with kouchi

Engagement review:

1. None of the kouchigari worked.

2. Combination from seoi to kouchi worked.

Conclusion:

Use combo seoi to kouchi against Yasuhiro Yamashita
at next tournament.

Suggestions:

1. If you have a problem with a left-handed competitor,
    practice with left-handers. Have them try the same
    types of offenses and defenses with you, and attune
    your body to adjust to them. Build defenses and
    offenses.

2. If you know that a certain competitor whom you will
    have to face is weak on the mat, practice mat work
    and takedowns.

3. If you've been losing your grip, review your videotapes
    and look for the precise moment when you seem to

lose control. Ask yourself if it is physical strength that is beating you. If so, then lift weights to augment your strength. Is it poor movement? Then practice to correct it.

4. Has a certain technique been failing you recently? Maybe you need to learn a new combination for entering into the technique. Maybe you need more *uchikomis* or more concentration. Practice for it.

5. Count the number of throws you perform during an average workout. Try to increase the number or intensity of your throws.

6. Practice nothing but a certain segment of judo—preferably one that you need to improve—during a workout. For example, during a workout practice nothing but *ashiwaza* (foot throws), *shimewaza* (chokes), grips, armbars, etc.

7. Develop a new technique. Be creative but practical.

8. Increase your cardiovascular output to 90 percent during your workout.

ANTON GEESINK

WERELDKAMPIOEN JUDO

1961

Even the great Anton Geesink had to leave Holland, his home country, and travel to Japan to learn judo. In the 1990s, Japanese *judoka* must travel from Japan to other countries in order to learn enough judo to keep up with the rest of the world.

"TABI"

In ancient Japan, when a young man wanted to become strong, he had to find a person who could teach him skills that would increase his strength. To do this, he embarked on a journey to find a master from whom he could learn. This practice was common and was referred to as *"tabi ni dekakeru"* (go out on a crusade). If in his travels he found such a master, he had to determine if the master would accept him as a student. The duration of apprenticeship depended on the master's and the student's abilities. Once the student learned all he could from the master, he would most likely move on to another master. Some students became excellent swordsmen and were hired to instruct *daimyo* and *shogun* and their armies. Others remained perpetual students seeking excellence through other *sensei* (teachers).

We all go on our quests, seeking sensei, situations, championships and successes in life. May you find the success you are looking for as you travel this way, the *ju-do* (gentle way).

Studying experimental rats is an excellent way to understand human behavior. Let's say we do a three-week-long experiment with a dozen rats. Half of them are trained to jump in response to an electric stimulus. The other half are left alone to do nothing. At the onset of the experiment, all twelve rats are fairly identical.

Upon completion of the experiment, there will be noticeable changes in the muscles and nerves of the trained rats, specifically:
1. an increase in muscle fiber size in the hind legs,
2. an increase in the number of nerve cells and synapses which carry electrochemical messages,
3. and an increase in motor-end plates (nerve cells that attach to the muscles and carry the impulses).

In addition, in the trained rats there will most likely be an increase in the amount of neurotransmitters—for example, acetylcholine, acetylcholinesterase, serotonin, epinephrine, norepinephrine, etc.—which are the chemicals that send messages across the synapse of the brain. All these increases help improve performance.

The rats that were left alone will show no changes.

When we place stress on our bodies, we will also have increases in performance specific to the type of stress we placed on our bodies. This is called the SAID principle, which means Specific Adaptations to Imposed Demands. Therefore, doing entry drills for an *uchimata* (inner thigh throw) won't improve your mat work.

The more you execute a specific movement, the better it will get. It's truly a case of "use it or lose it." Some "new age" coaches feel that *uchikomis* are a waste of time. Most likely, it's all in how one works on the uchikomis that will determine whether or not they are beneficial. If you perform your uchikomis apathetically, these may not be as beneficial as when they are practiced under realistic conditions. Here, stress becomes a catalyst to success.

Photo courtesy of Judo Journal

Yasuhiro Yamashita (facing forward), is pictured here executing *uchikomis* (entry drills) at L.A. Tenri *dojo*.

Former U.S. Champion and U.S. International Coach Irwin Cohen had this to say about *randori:* "Some competitors don't know the difference between randori and *shiai* (tournaments). They let their egos get in the way and now they don't want to get thrown—ever. They freeze up and place emphasis on defense. If a guy is getting countered, that means he's trying."

In randori, you should be looser and take chances. It's a time for experimentation and learning, not a time to see who is the best competitor. It's a time to see if you can "outslick" rather than overpower your opponent. It's a time to develop a throw to the opposite side. It's a time to see how little strength you can use and still defeat your opponent. It's a time to develop combinations. It's a time to develop those twisting, turning, slipping, jamming, tugging, hugging, dancing movements you really don't learn until you apply your techniques while moving about under stressful conditions. It's a time to develop your cardiovascular conditioning. In shiai, on the other hand, all your efforts—physical, emotional and mental—are required. It's time to do battle.

Photo by Hayward Nishioka

Competitors at the Olympic Training Center in Colorado Springs, Colorado, are shown getting ready for the U.S. International Invitational Championships with a light warm-up and workout.

Photo by Hayward Nishioka

Judoka and Ultimate Fighter "Ghetto Joe" Charles,
halfway through a judo workout.

HAVE YOU WORKED OUT?

How hard have you worked out? How hard have you *really* worked out? Have you worked out until your judo *gi* was soaked? Have you worked out until your belt was soaked? Have you worked out until salt crystals formed lightly around your mouth and face as your perspiration evaporated? Have you worked out until you could see your own body heat rising like smoke? Have you worked out until your whole body ached and all you wanted to do was to sleep it off? Have you worked out until you could not even stand up? Have you worked out until your body no longer had energy and you felt like your opponent sloshed you around like a wet towel mopping up the floor? Well, have you worked out? If so, how often?

We all would like to progress at a consistent pace, and in many endeavors we progress at regular intervals. In judo, however, the road to improvement is paved with ups, downs and plateaus.

During some workouts, you're able to pin, toss, choke and armbar everyone in sight. On other days, nothing works. During these "nothing works" days, *judoka* sometimes get discouraged and quit. This is unfortunate, since what they are experiencing during these times is a temporary barrier that, once broken through, makes them better judoka.

The Japanese word for these setbacks, which in English are called "slumps," is *su-ram-pu*. In Japanese, when someone asks someone about how he feels, he says *"Choshi wa doo?"* If the person questioned feels good, he answers *"Choshi ga ii."* If he feels bad, he answers *"Choshi ga waruii."*

While we often feel that anything bad or negative is something completely bad that will never change, the Japanese tend to view anything bad or negative as a point in time that won't stay bad but will soon surge forward and eventually become good. It's the proverbial "half-full, half-empty" attitude.

A *su-ram-pu* may last a month or two, or even longer. These slumps may occur as a result of a negative perception you have of your progress. However, others may not regard your progress in the same manner. In effect, your slump may be just in your head.

One remedy is to have someone objectively evaluate your progress during practice. For example, he can evaluate the number of times you executed an *ippon* (one-armed throw against a tough opponent), or how may times you were able to avoid or counter your opponent's attempt to throw you.

If you are discouraged about your progress and are wondering if you should quit, you should write in your journal what you think the barrier is, and then determine practical steps to overcome it. Sometimes capturing your thoughts on paper helps you analyze the problem.

The alternative is to quit and later resume practice, only to find that those whom you easily handled before have in the interim progressed and are now easily handling you. But, strangely enough, sometimes it's the best thing to do. Stop for a while, rest, then come back. It's funny how sometimes you can take a break, come back, and beat the pants off of whomever you work out with.

Photo © Bob Willingham, 1998

Sometimes you feel like you're not making any progress. In fact it seems as if things are getting worse. This feeling is usually referred to as a "slump." This often occurs before a big surge forward. So don't give up.

Photo by Margaret George

Some instructors don't like you to visit other *dojo* because they don't want to lose you as a student and they don't want you to give away secret techniques. However, judo instructors at Los Angeles City College encourage their students to visit other dojo to broaden their knowledge of and proficiency in judo.

DOJO HOPPING   1.18

In *dojo* (training hall) hopping, there are some written and unwritten rules. Here are some suggestions:

1. Read the dojo's written rules.

2. Watch the practice session first.

3. Always ask the head *sensei* for permission to practice.

4. Always have the right attitude; not one that is smug, cocky or bullish.

5. Be judicious with weaker persons; be aggressive with stronger persons.

6. Make sure to work with those that are particularly strong.

See what makes them so strong. Is it their size, strength, technique, speed, flexibility or cardiovascular ability? Once you know, figure out what you must do to offset their strength.

7. Ask the opinion of your own instructor.

8. Go to learn, not to show off.

9. Always say "Thank you" after practice.

10. Write down your perceptions of the dojo and the practice sessions in your journal.

A young student asked noted martial artist Cheng Man Ching, "What of studying with other masters?" Ching answered, "I would have to think very little of my art if I didn't want it compared to somebody else's."

At night as you are about to fall asleep, imagine either a flashing light or a steady periodic beat. Now try initiating an entry into a throw between the flashes of light or the beat. Thus, flash or beat—enter!—flash or beat—enter!—flash or beat. Make your mental body move through space without being hit by light or sound waves.

In the beginning, these flashes may be slow and these images may be hazy. With time, these images will become more vivid and may possibly be in color. And your body may respond with sudden, involuntary jerks.

You may even anticipate the pulse or beat and may enter simultaneously to fit in just as its pulse ends. Now, make the pulse or beat appear randomly without a definite rhythm to key in on. Then extend the period of concentration beyond a couple of minutes. Who said mental practice was easy? Think! Go! Beep, beep, beep, beep, beep, beep, beep, ...

Photo courtesy of Hayward Nishioka

Kinesiological studies indicate that reviewing a skill over
and over again in your mind will enhance performance.

American inventor Thomas Edison slept only three hours a night, but he took little catnaps during the day. Still others require the normal 7 to 8 hours.

What's disconcerting is when you can't sleep just prior to a competition. The night before a tournament you toss and flop about your bed, unable to sleep. What do you do? How about an onion sandwich and a glass of milk? How about a heavy meal before bed? Nope, have to make weight tomorrow. Sex? No, too tiring and takes away the edge. Sleeping pills? No, it's a banned substance. How about pre-planning? Pre-planning? Hmmm.

In addition to pre-tournament jitters, elite athletes must deal with the fact that they travel through time zones, sometimes three or more, right before a major tournament. Plan on arriving at the tournament site a couple of days early to let your body and brain readjust to the time difference. It's a waste of time, effort and finances to travel over land and sea to arrive drained on the day of competition. If the trip is short in duration, don't sleep as much as you normally do for two days prior to a competition. That way, sleep should be a welcome occurrence the day before competition. In any event, you want to approximate your normal sleep pattern as best you can.

Researchers claim that we toss and turn as many as forty to sixty times a night and fall in and out of four stages of sleep, needing less and less of the fourth, third and second stages. REM sleep, or the lightest stage, is characterized by Rapid Eye Movements (the eyeball under the closed eyelid moves to and fro). This stage is usually when dreams occur. Deprivation of REM sleep causes edginess. Well, what's so bad about that? Now, there's yet another reason to beat up your opponents. After all, they caused you to lose sleep.

Photo by Hayward Nishioka

U.S. World and Olympic Judo Team member Damon Keeve, taking a nap. He is traveling through several time zones, and this is his attempt to be refreshed for an upcoming tournament.

Photo by Kelly Barnes

Competitors in a judo tournament are shown carbo-loading before their respective matches. Watch your weight.

CARBO-LOADING 1.21

It's always intriguing to see athletes who are geared toward competition and the development of their bodies to their fullest potential seek the secret formula that will give them superhuman powers (the Flubber syndrome). Ben Johnson's big sin was that he got caught. There are others. Whatever the International Olympic Committee misseth, Mother Nature catcheth.

We should know what is best for our bodies in the long run and not use anabolic steroids and ergogenic aids just for short-term gains.

If we look at natural foods that aid performance, Dr. Peter Van from the Olympic Training Center in Colorado Springs says, "Carbohydrates are the best source of energy for athletes." The best sources for carbohydrates are pastas, fruits and vegetables. Proteins and fats take longer to translate into a usable energy source.

The body utilizes energy in the following priority order, with some overlaps into each area:

1. stored glycogen in the muscle tissue
2. carbohydrates
3. fats
4. proteins

"Fartlek." Now there's a word for you. It always elicits a queer sense of humor in me. If I say the word, will people know what I'm talking about? Will they also feel funny and wonder how they should respond? In other words, do I dare say the word at a formal dinner? Maybe, if I was in Sweden.

"Fartlek" means "speed play." Runners utilize fartlek training to help increase their performance. Since this type of workout simulates the rhythm of *randori* sessions, this could be beneficial for *judoka* as well.

Fartlek training is done by running unevenly—sometimes swiftly, sometimes slowly, sometimes all-out—but never stopping, for at least 20 minutes at a time. The course may vary; it could be an uneven mountain path, or a street, or a field, etc. As often as you are able, you should sprint all-out to give your cardiovascular system a work-out. Since you run at least 20 minutes or more at a time, this workout is aerobic. When random sprints are incorporated into the workout, it is anaerobic as well.

For those of you who are bored to tears with jogging, try fartleking around. You'll get into shape faster than by just jogging.

Photo courtesy of Hayward Nishioka

Oleg Zatsepin, going through the motions of *fartlek* training, racing to catch up with the student in front of him.

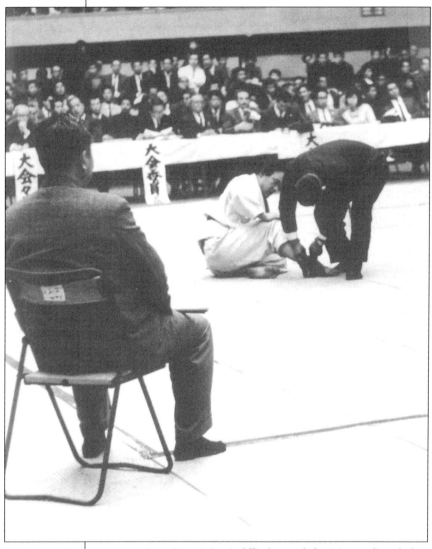

Assessing an injury is difficult enough, but it is complicated when pressures to succeed could cause an athlete to suffer from injuries that are considered to be psychosomatic.

INJURY EXCUSES   1.23

"I wasn't able to do as well because of my injury." "If I wasn't injured, I could have beaten him easily." "My injured arm prevented me from entering into my favorite throw." "I was able to defeat him despite my injury. See my bandages!"

While injuries will occur, it's probably prudent not to work out if doing so will aggravate them. Furthermore, it could be psychologically damaging if you use your injury as a crutch for losses sustained, a hedge against possible defeat, or even an instrument of self-martyrdom.

If you are suffering from a severe injury, you shouldn't compete. Your body and your brain will tell you what to do. If you go into shock and your inner voice hollers "Oh, S...!" you should probably stop. But if it's just a little owwie, don't be a baby.

The biggest problem that coaches, parents and players need to understand is that an injury may be symptomatic of a psychological problem rather than a physical one. That could become chronic, either psychologically or psychosomatically. Usually, this happens when you over-load your child with demands that are beyond his means. He figures that an injury is the only honorable way to get out of a situation that, as a young child, he need only cry to get out of.

Sometimes in the pursuit of excellence we are blind to what we really should be achieving, which is building, not breaking, another human being. Granted, this is a difficult line to discern. It is raised here so that we may be aware of this issue as a potential for growth or a potential for regression.

My favorite *gi,* my lucky belt, my lucky underwear. I've got to have steak the night before a tournament. No sex for a month before a major tournament. Fruit punch after weigh-in. Go to church for a month of Sundays. Get up on the right side of the bed. Avoid black cats. Don't step on sidewalk lines.

What if I told you they all work? Then do it. What if I told you they had nothing to do with performance? Then don't do it!

The only thing I don't like about superstitions is rabbit's feet. Think of all the poor bunnies who lost their feet over silly superstitions.

During the 1950s and 1960s, people thought that rabbit's-foot keychains were supposed to bring good luck. Now they'll bring animal rights activists to your door.

U.S. Olympian Steven Seck is shown here coaching blind student Lyn Manning. Manning, a former Los Angeles City College student, won a silver medal at the 1995 Judo World Championships in a special division comprised of *judoka* who are handicapped.

MAPPING OUT YOUR CONTESTS — 1.25

It's amazing that some competitors don't want to know who their opponents are until they arrive at the tournament site or at matside. One player remarked, "If I know who I have to play in the first round, tomorrow I may not get any sleep if his name happens to be Yasuhiro Yamashita."

Other competitors will map out their strategy, allowing for every possible contingency. One such competitor may think, "In pool A, I have all the weaker players. The tough ones are in Pool B. Now, let's see, I know I can get past the first guy. I don't know the second guy. I'll watch his match after I fight my first round. The third guy is a pretty good stand-up fighter, but on the mat he's mine. Now, the fourth guy is hot and cold. I'll check him out today and see. He's cold! OK."

Former U.S. Champion, Olympian and physical educator Steven Seck has this to say about mapping out a strategy: "It's important to be aware of whom you're going to fight so you mentally prepare game plans." As a competitor, Steven was always at matside watching his next opponent, looking for strengths and weaknesses. He's still doing so in the 1990s, but as a coach. He continues: "A will probably beat B; he's your next opponent. Beat A and you'll breeze through your pool. The other pool is weak—you can beat any one of them." Be cautious when you plan your strategy. Don't get too cocky!

It's difficult to beat up someone you have never met before. Your opponent may be good-natured, good-looking and personable, but for four or five minutes he's going to be your worst enemy. He can be your friend the rest of the day, but now he's in your way.

How do you do it? Get mad! At what? Look for something irritating about your opponent: his shoes, his clothes, his breath, his body odor, his attitude, his friends or his cockiness (which will only be magnified if he defeats you). Find the fault and key in on it. Make it the reason why you would want to beat up your opponent.

Former U.S. Grand Champion Gene LeBell once saw a major opponent smoking a cigar, and he decided he couldn't lose to a smoker. He went out and dusted him. Former Olympian and U.S. Grand Champion Pat Burris always found a reason to hate his opponent. "It's that guy on the other side causing me all this anguish, and he's going to have to pay for it!" Burris said.

After you're done, don't forget to turn off the fault-finding switch.

CRASH and BURN STUNT TEAM

To Hayward The Great

LET US ALL TEAM UP AND WISH
Season Greetings and a Happy
New Year to You and Yours.

Gene LeBell

Gene LeBell is one of America's toughest *judoka* and stuntmen.

Photo by Hayward Nishioka

Leo White (top) is considered by many people to be the "iron horse" of judo. He is giving his opponent an attitude adjustment. Leo retired in 1997 at age 37 after winning 13 national championships, and being a member of two Olympic teams. As a competitor, he has beaten Robert Van de Walle of Belgium and Stephane Traineau of France.

PREPPING 1.27

Slap, slap, pat, pat, jump, jump, the sign of the cross. What is he talking about?

U.S. National Champion and Olympian Leo White once remarked, "Have you ever noticed how competitors at matside prepare themselves to do battle?" Competitors have their teammates slap them on their backs and hamstrings. Or how about those guys who slap their face with their hand as if they needed to wake up further? Koreans have been known to step up on the mat, jump up, and slam their two feet down on the mat a couple of times like they are stomping on a pile of bugs.

Imagine what these bizarre actions must look like to the unaccustomed eye. Are these people nuts or something? No, not really. It is just a ritual competitors do to call up that extra something deep down inside or somewhere out there to awaken the element that gives them the edge. For others, it may be merely a mental button they need to push to get things started. "In the name of the Father, Son, and the Holy Ghost, *hajime* (begin)! Hyaaa!"

Is it better to have a lot of techniques in your arsenal, or just one good one? What if you know only one technique really well and it fails? What backup techniques do you have? Then again, what if you are able to perform a lot of techniques, but you don't know them sufficiently enough to overcome your opponent? It takes time to learn a technique. Is it better to concentrate your energy on one technique, or diffuse your energy over six or seven moves?

I once witnessed a demonstration in which a couple of would-be assailants attacked a slightly built man. This man suddenly exploded into a whirlwind of punches and kicks. He must have hit each of his opponents at least seven to ten times. Naturally, they lost. I was astonished by the speed and sequence of blows showered upon them.

A friend then commented, "The guy must not be too good if he has to expend that much energy to do what could be done in one or two blows. Wouldn't it be neat if we had one punch or kick that we could execute on anyone, and it was so surefire that if we were to try it 100 times against a defending opponent it would work 100 times?" The choice is yours.

Hayward Nishioka (right), throwing Tony Owed during a tournament in 1965.

Photo by Hayward Nishioka

After they competed at the U.S. International Invitational Championships, hundreds of elite *judoka* came together to learn and practice high-level judo at the International Training Camp held at the U.S. Olympic Training Center in Colorado Springs, Colorado.

"If you want a tiger's cub, you must enter the tiger's den."

The cub represents the idea of being or becoming a champion. The den, of course, is the training area where you attain the tools to become a champion.

Whether the den happens to be a local *dojo*, or perhaps a major judo center in Japan or Europe, it's tough to go through rough training sessions over an extended period of time. This is especially true in Japan, where you might walk into a dojo and find 40 or 50 black belts ready and willing to rip your head off your shoulder just for the amusement of watching you walk funny.

Every *judoka* who aspires to greatness knows he has to seek out those training centers and jump in and hone his skills. No one is a champion from day one. Everyone needs bodies to train with. Everyone is tempered in fire and water. Everyone enters the den if he wants a tiger's cub.

Have you ever noticed how some moments in time are so relaxed? Ensconced in your easy chair, you sip a cool beverage and listen to elevator music, impervious to the rest of the world's trouble. Yet at other moments your palms are sweating, your heart is beating so hard it feels as if it is about to burst, your breathing is heavy, and your brain and body are stressed. You ask yourself, "Should I go for it or should I stop?" knowing all the while that making the wrong decision will affect the rest of your life. Worse yet is not knowing that making the wrong decision will affect the rest of your life.

This makes me think about the fate of competitors who fall prey to the silver medal syndrome. These players, for some reason or another, just don't quite make it to the top. They get through the semifinals and suddenly say to themselves, "Whatever I do from now on, I'll at least have no less than a silver medal." Now a silver medal is not bad, and it is further than everyone else except one person has been able to progress. If you've fought your heart and soul out and fate was not on your side this time, it's OK.

It's not OK, however, if you said, "Wow, this is further than anyone else got." It's not OK if you were starry-eyed and said, "What am I doing in the finals?" It's not OK if you don't compete 100 percent and go for the gold. You don't make it to within striking distance of the gold medal every day. Some people get only one chance to go for the gold, and if you're in that position you've got to know that it is a critical moment. You've got to go for the gold and not be satisfied with second place.

In Japanese, there is a saying *"ichigo ichi,"* which means "one time, one meeting." There are moments in time that are critical, for they may open an avenue to success only one time. Take them! They may be the only times all the elements of fate will be meeting like this.

Isao Inokuma (right) with his teacher Watanabe *sensei*. Inokuma didn't miss his critical moments. He was All-Japan champion twice, as well as a world and Olympic champion. In the 1990s, he is the president of his own construction company.

"KUGEI"

工芸

We all start with the first step. We all must develop two
arms, two legs, a body and a brain.

Arms, legs, a body, a brain. Put them into a judo *gi* and what do you have? Why are some people better than others? Why did someone who looked like Rambo lose to the guy who looks like Ichabod Crane? How did a 150-pound champion come in second in the All-Japan Championships when his opponents' average weight was 225 pounds? Of course, more often than not, the bigger guy wins. But still, why are there these anomalies, these exceptions to the rule? What do these people possess that others do not? Is it more brains? More muscles? More spirit? More luck? More techniques?

What are the ingredients for success? Was the combination of mental and physical training just right? Was a good coach available? Was there desire? Great family support? Perhaps the person was a natural athlete. Are some more suited for judo than others? Are champions born or made?

Arms, legs, a body, a brain.

"Semeru" means "press on" or "attack." General George S. Patton was once asked why he never retreated. He answered, "I don't like to pay for the same real estate twice." Another general, upon landing on foreign soil, burned his ships. When asked why, he replied that there was now only one way to go: forward.

In judo, the battle is usually won by the aggressor. In fact, you are penalized if you don't do anything. How many times should you attack during a five-minute match? Usually, you should attack or attempt to attack with a throw once every twenty or thirty seconds. That translates into ten to fifteen times during a five-minute match. If you can press the attack even further to enter at every opportunity or be in your opponent's face constantly, you and your opponent will know the meaning of "semeru."

When you are pressing the attack, you may not necessarily be attempting throw after throw. Instead, it may be that you can't find an opening, but that you are keeping up the pressure, turning up the steam, keeping your opponent to the edge, pressing him into the corner, and giving him no chance to think about attacking. In a manner of speaking, you are the aggressor and he is the prey. You are not decreasing the pressure or allowing him to possibly reverse roles. Do you get the picture? Now get the opponent!

Photo by Hayward Nishioka

Never give up trying to throw.
Never give up trying to get away.
Never, never give up.

The first thing anyone does is learn to fall correctly. Next is how to throw. For illustrative purposes, John Ogden *sensei* instructs his class.

FIRST LEVELS OF THROWS   2.3

Usually, a beginner is taught to throw first from a static position and via a step-by-step process. Step one, step across with your right foot with your arm around your opponent's waist. Step two, bend your knees and pull your opponent forward. Step three, throw your hip across. Step four, bring your second foot back. Step five, lift and pull your opponent over. *Voilà!*—an *ogoshi* (hip throw).

Randori?! You mean try to throw my opponent while moving, while defending, while worrying about what to do about these four steel bars between us we call arms? Yeah, right!

There's an opening. There's another. And another. But how do I get my body to do step one before my opponent moves out of position?

Ask *sensei.* Answer from sensei: "Practice, practice, practice!"

"Ah! It's happening. I'm throwing. Ugh, not perfectly, but he's going over. The throws are a little messy, but they're basically pretty good."

To progress beyond this level, you need to possess several qualities common to all champions. Some champions have a strong desire to win and utilize throwing techniques as a means to an end. Some receive a "high" from having executed a beautiful throw. Whatever triggers the need to throw, it must be celebrated.

You have to get a "high" from throwing. Your body has natural opiates, called endorphins, that when released make you feel good. Runners call this feeling the "runner's high." *Judoka* also get these highs from throwing. However, we don't think about them as much and often dismiss them with a simple "Humph, that felt pretty good" when we should be saying "Yeah!"

Shown here is Hayward Nishioka at the 1968 Nationals trying to throw Yoshinori Itoh of Japan. Shigero Tashima is the referee.

All-Japan, World and Olympic gold medalist Isao Okano explodes
again into the "time of heaven."

HIGHER LEVELS OF THROWS   2.5

At some point you will execute a throw, look down at your devastated opponent, and say to yourself, "How did he get down there? I don't recall having thrown him."

Sometimes a throw is an event in slow motion. You see your opponent moving in slow motion while you take advantage of him at regular speed.

One of the most interesting levels to attain is one in which nothing can go wrong. Tsutomu Ohshima, a famous karate *sensei,* referred to it as the "Time of Heaven." This is that instant in time when all the conditions in the universe are at your disposal. While you are thinking about going from point A to point B with a *seoinage* (shoulder throw), your body is already there. Your opponent looks to twist out, but you have already made the adjustments to land him on his back. As you finish the throw, you wake to the reality that some seemingly outside force has flawlessly guided your action.

These levels are attained only from diligent practice, when desire comes from inside yourself. The higher levels are there for those who search for them.

Should you learn many techniques, or should you concentrate on only one technique? If you know many techniques, you can revert to others if one fails until the right one defeats your opponent.

Maybe the answer lies in knowing how to perform a technique so well that it works no matter who your opponent is.

For many, the answer will lie somewhere in-between. You will have a favorite throw, or *tokui waza,* and a couple of set-up throws or support throws at your disposal.

Tokui wazas are your bread-and-butter techniques that you feel comfortable executing. You know when to enter into the throw, how to maneuver your opponent into position, and how to crash-land him if he is about to take flight.

A *judoka* is executing a *sumigaeshi* (sacrifice throw) on his opponent
for a full-point score. His opponent is vertical and twisting on his head
to avoid landing on his back.

U.S. Collegiate champion Luis Gonzales (top) gives everything he has to win this match. At this moment, he is focused on nothing else but what needs to be done to win.

LOSING THE SELF

Act! Don't act! As long as you're conscious of your every move, trying to act like someone else, holding back and not going all-out, or thinking about what to do rather than doing it, you're not there yet.

When you're in shape and know how to pace yourself, let go of yourself and focus completely on executing your techniques. Don't think about how you're moving or what you're doing. Just do it. All your energy should be directed into pure aggression.

Leave no space for extraneous thoughts. Don't be thinking, "What do I look like? What's for dinner? What about my injured toe?" It takes practice to remove that second of reservation that divides winners from losers. It takes only a second of reservation and doubt to lose a match.

Although judo is not a sport in which you may live or die for lack of decisiveness, it has its roots in survival. Your survival may be dependent, ironically, on your ability to disregard yourself and say, "Whether I die or not, I'm going to do this," or to do something with such concentration and intensity that there is no room for other thoughts.

2.8 THE ULTIMATE THROW

Have you ever thought about what you consider to be the ultimate throw? I thought about this when I was young, and determined that my ultimate throw would be one I could execute with so much intensity that it would render my opponent unconscious when he hit the mat.

To many people, perhaps, this might seem like an unreasonable thing to do. Nonetheless, let's look at what it takes to accomplish a throw against an unwilling opponent. Do you need speed? Impact? Drive and willpower? "A need to succeed"? Do you need to hate to lose? If your answer is "Yes," then one of the ways to get there is to use the principle of overload. In other words, do more than what is necessary or seemingly reasonable.

Two *judoka* are "toe-dancing." Only this is nothing like any ballet I've seen before.

Oliver Pang photo

Hayward Nishioka (left) vs. Yuzo Koga (right) at the 1965 Nationals.

WHEN DO I ATTACK? 2.9

Remember when you first started to *randori*? You had just learned a new throw, and you were going to use it on a poor, unsuspecting opponent. Wrong! Your attacks will come only after many attempts and many hours of devoted practice to train your body to react to openings in your opponent's weaknesses.

But you must start somewhere. So where do you start? With the first step!

1. Know what kind of shape you are in so you know how much energy you have to expend within the given time frame.

2. Attack as much as you can without tiring out in the first few minutes. Push yourself, but not to instant exhaustion.

3. If you have problems accomplishing any throws, try:

   a. working with weaker opponents,

   b. doing throw for throws, or

   c. doing semi-tough workouts with less resistance. If a thrower gets in a good one, study it.

   d. If you get in a good one, try getting another one then another and another.

From Japan's Saigo Shiro's legendary *yama arashi* (mountain-storm throw) to Poland's Beata Maksymow's *uchimata,* every major player has a *tokui waza* (favorite technique) whether it's a pin, choke, armbar or throw.

It's difficult to say how you come to select a specific technique to be your tokui waza. Perhaps you see it performed spectacularly, desire to emulate the performance, then execute it and find it comfortable. Maybe it's the only throw your instructor teaches you. Well, now it's time for a change. You want to have a new tokui waza, but how do you develop one?

First, you have to badly want to execute this new throw. So badly that you will dig deep down in your soul and commit your body to learn it no matter what obstacles stand in your way. Then do the following:

1. Mentally picture the throw you want to perform. Picture it performed to the side, front, other side, back, top, and at a three-quarter angle, then slowly place yourself inside the mental moving image. Feel it.

2. Now try it as you see it at its best. Do static *uchikomis* at least two hundred to one thousand times to get comfortable with the throw. Do the technique slowly and correctly in the beginning. Incorrect execution will develop incorrect nerve patterns, which will decrease your movement time and make it difficult to relearn later.

3. Once you have a feel for the throw, perform it with more speed. Next, do it while you and your opponent are moving.

4. Your opponent should first cooperate with you, then make it increasingly difficult—but never impossible—

for you to throw him.

5. Now try the throw doing *randori* sessions with people you can easily throw. Use only the throw you're trying to develop. It may be wise to take falls for them, too. Otherwise, they'll lose interest in working with you and you'll lose partners.

6. Gradually work toward tougher opponents as you develop your confidence.

7. When you're comfortable with this new throw and are using it easily, that's it. You have a new tokui waza.

8. When your opponents build a tolerance for your tokui waza, it's time to develop a new one.

Two *judoka* in search of their respective *tokui waza*.
Rick Celloto is the referee.

Ulla Werbrouck of Belgium (right) dodges Japan's Yoko Tanabe's (left) *uchimata* (inner thigh throw) and hurls her to the ground for the *ippon*, (full point), the match victory and the Olympic gold medal.

I CAN SEE CLEARLY NOW

Novice players don't see movement as clearly as advanced players. This is why they are easily caught. Novice players are too busy defending and contracting everything to move themselves or see movement. As you advance, an evolution occurs: you can defend better, move better, and utilize your energy and muscles more efficiently. As you develop these factors, you will be able to focus on the movements in front of you.

Actually, you will begin to see with your body. Your body will sense your opponent's movements from just your grip. Your opponent's movements will tell you when to attack. Your body will move before your brain engages, allowing you to react appropriately to the situation. You are making sense of these patterns with your body and are developing an image in your mind. As you develop this ability, your efforts become coordinated and your reliance on your other senses becomes keener. It is a lot like playing video games. Do you see what I mean?

When you view beginners struggling during a *randori* session, you often notice something different about their body movement. Their bodies, especially their arms, are usually more rigid, and their movements are more erratic. Each novice seems to dance on his toes. Their arms are outstretched and stiff, and their bodies are bent over in an extreme defensive posture. Most likely, their eyes are dilated.

On the other hand, advanced players seemingly float through their workouts. Their breathing is regulated; their muscles are contracted, yet not so much that it inhibits their ability to attack; and their posture is fairly upright, enabling them to defend with just the slightest bend in the knees or twist of the hip. They look immovable as they dance about and throw everyone.

In reference to this settled state when one is at ease with the confrontation and "the hips are settled," the Japanese say *"koshi ga suwatte iru."* This is the state that enables *judoka* to succeed. Reaching this level requires long hours of practice, but once you are there, you'll know it. You won't have to use 100 percent of your strength to practice your judo.

Photo by Hayward Nishioka

Offense and defense are better facilitated by the correct use of the hips
rather than just the reliance on strong arms.

Perfect.

PERFECT

In golf, when you drive a ball just right a "crack" sounds as the ball disappears. You feel it in your arms and all over your body. The same is true of baseball when a player hits a home run, in football when one makes a perfect tackle, or in diving when one performs a perfect entry into the pool. Some techniques are just "perfect" and are executed almost effortlessly.

Judo throws are very similar. Once you've performed a perfect judo throw, your body knows something that many people will never understand. It was effortless, sudden, decisive, awesome and perfect.

SECOND EFFORT 2.14

Once, while watching *Monday Night Football*, I saw a halfback get handed the ball. He then ran for the line, whereupon he was met by a guard, a tackle and part of the center. As they impacted, there was a sudden pause in forward motion. Then, without capitulation, the halfback's feet dug in and ran again, this time going over the top. "Touchdown!"

There are also moments of second effort in judo. And they are often what separates the successful player from the average player. In 1990 I watched Yael Arad of Israel execute a right *osotogari*. Her opponent stopped her attack, but Arad quickly followed up with a left *kosoto-gake* (inside major reap) for an *ippon* (one point). In the 1988 Olympics, Michael Swain tried a *tomoe nage* (stomach throw) against his opponent and missed. Undaunted, he continued and fought his opponent on the mat and, after considerable effort, finally pinned him. Johnny Hobales had been trying to win the U.S. Senior Nationals for years, but he came up short every time. However, he did not give up. In 1990, he became national champion.

If at first you don't succeed, try again.

U.S. Champion Johnny Hobales (right) follows up with a leg grab after having applied and failed at one technique.

I'm going to share with you something that happened to me when I was young. I was at a friend's house when suddenly someone burst the door open and threw a young lady to the floor. I got up to assist her, then turned to the person who threw her down. I remember saying, "What?" and then—Pow! Before I could say anything else I was sailing from the living room to the kitchen and sliding on the floor, abruptly stopping against a cabinet door. My face was numb, and a raw feeling gripped me. I got up barely in time to get out of the way of this charging 190-pounder, who was yelling in rage incoherently for me to get out and mind my own business. As he ran toward me I jerkily sidekicked him, and I felt my foot slice in and crack something in his rib cage. He kept coming. I backhanded him and his head rocked backward, but he kept coming. He tackled me, and we went to the ground. I pinned him using a *kamishiho* and miraculously he escaped. Punching and flailing, I found myself with my feet between my opponent and me, my back against the floor. He was on top dripping blood from his nose. I had clearly been getting the better of him, but he wouldn't stop.

In that moment, after all I had done to dissuade him from his aggression, he was intent on his objective even if it killed him. In that instant I realized that this was a fight to the death. It was his life or mine. If I killed him I would lose and be scarred for life. But if he killed me the game would be over ... all over.

In the background, my friend and her roommate were in hysterics, screaming at us and calling the police. Out of breath, he finally said, "Are you getting out now?" Before my brain kicked in, my mouth said, "Yes," and I left with my friend.

Later, I found out that the individual had been drinking and felt no pain. The girl he flung down was his girlfriend. And he was a streetfighter from a local gang with little respect for life.

This event had a profound effect on me. It brought me close to death, and made me understand that if you are going to do something—to reach some goal—even if it might kill you, you have great power. It's that "even if it kills me" syndrome.

I wonder what kind of techniques would evolve out of our workouts if we used this syndrome each time we entered into our technique, or used it in our workouts, tournaments, work or lives. The ancient samurai used to say, "You must throw down your life in order to find it."

Photo by Hayward Nishioka

"I'm going to do this even if it kills me!" says U.S. Champion Dave Faulkner (right). In desperation, Faulkner arches in an effort to finish off a leg and his opponent.

Powel Nastula of Poland upends Kim Min-Soo of Korea to receive a *wazari* (half point). He quickly follows up with a pin for the other half-point. Nastula is noted for his wholehearted attempts that have helped him become European, World, and—in this photo—1996 Olympic judo gold medalist.

"OMOIKITTE"

In Japanese, *"omoi"* means "to think." *"Kiru"* is a verb meaning "to cut," the command form of which is *"kitte."* Together, they mean "Cut all thought of what you are doing." For the *judoka,* this is often an adverb describing how you should enter into a throw. In other words, don't worry about failure, and don't worry about counters. Don't think! Act! Propel yourself wholeheartedly into the throw.

If you're going to fail, you'll fail. If you're going to be countered, it will happen, but not without a wholehearted attempt on your part, is there a chance for success. Nothing should take precedence over doing the throw as if its the only thing that matters. Former U.S. Grand Champion Kazuo Shinohara once said, "If you expend 80 percent of your energy and fail in a throw, and come back out and try again using 100 percent and succeed, that's 180 percent. Wouldn't it have been more efficient to have used 100 percent effort and succeeded from the start?"

When practicing, if you listen to your inner self you can usually hear a voice saying, "It won't work," "Not now," "No," or "I can't attack." These inner words have to be cut out. You have to be able to hear these doubtful words first. Then, if you've practiced your techniques and *uchikomis,* cut the doubt and—*omoikitte*—apply them.

In the 1980s there has been an ever-growing awareness among *judoka* that new judo techniques are evolving. Now, in the new millennium, we hear instructors say, "That's not a judo throw!" or, "He doesn't know judo" less and less. Unfortunately, some instructors unwilling to accept change will remain in a cultural vacuum. They will not teach modern world and Olympic judo. Rather, they will teach basic judo in a recreational setting.

Of course, there is nothing wrong with basic judo. What becomes problematic is the bruised egos of instructors whose students sometimes, if not often, lose their matches because they are unaccustomed to the throws, pins, chokes, and armbars that *sensei* and coaches who study the latest developments in Olympic sport judo teach their students.

These sensei often take their bruised egos to the boardroom or association meeting and have their own contests, but without a referee or *shinban*. Only more astute sensei are able to separate the issues from their egos. Only true leaders will think of the progression of our wonderful sport rather than regress to the Japanese concept of *kataki uchi* (recrimination or retaliation), which is the idea that "I lost face so now I'll get even with him."

Judo is changing. It changed largely due to the existence of new rules that define what constitutes a win via a throw, pin, choke, armbar or decision. It defined rather than named. In fact, some throws have yet to be named. Some throws have yet to be discovered. It's exciting to await the birth of new techniques, because it means there is still room to grow.

We can't just stand around and watch someone get slammed to the mat on his back so hard that the impact registers 8.2 on the Richter scale, or watch someone get pinned so hard that the only things moving are his eyeballs, and say, "Well, that's not judo." Well, if it isn't judo and it's defeating judo, it's time to incorporate it and make it part of our sport. Let's make it a part of our changing judo.

Even in Japan, novel techniques are executed all the time. The only thing is, these techniques are usually categorized as variations *(kezure)*, but they are hardly ever given new names. This is a real problem when trying to visualize what someone is talking about.

Skydiving, the famous Maejima *kosoto*, sends his opponent smashing into the mat.

INVENTIVENESS

How many throws are there in judo? How many throws that really work are there in judo? Have new throws been invented? What distinguishes the various throws? How many more can be invented? When do you know you've done something new? What do you call a new throw? Is it enough to say it's a *kuzure* (modified technique)?

Since judo has become a worldwide sport, with *judoka* from various nations fighting each other for superiority, new techniques have arisen from various points of the globe. Often, these innovative throws do not exactly fit the mold of the traditional *gokyo no waza* (a classification of about forty basic judo throws), the same 126 techniques found in Mifune Kyuzo's book *Canon of Judo* or the 65 recognized throws of the *Kodokan*.

Since the classical techniques were cataloged, other countries have brought in new techniques from similar sports, invented new techniques, or at the very least brought in new entries into old techniques.

Some examples of this are the Korean *seoinage*, the Cuban seoinage, the *khabarelli* (back-somersault throw), the Korean *sukuinage* (scooping throw), the Korean *kanibasami* (crab-scissors throw), the Neil Adams armbar and the Micky Matsumoto tuck-and-roll armbar, to name a few. Although these techniques can't be found in traditional judo books, they enable their users to catch their opponents off-guard with throws or mat work to which no defenses have yet been developed.

Be inventive. Get your name on a new technique. Why not?

The old-timers say *koka* (technical advantage) judo is not judo! Like it or not, koka judo is here to stay. In the "old days," they brag, "We only had *wazaris* (half-points) and *ippons*." Oftentimes, even if a contestant consistently knocked his opponent to the mat, unless there was at least a wazari, the match was either a *hikiwake* (draw match) or it went into overtime. It wasn't uncommon for championship bouts to last 15 to 20 minutes due to successive two-minute overtimes. Whoever pooped out first lost the match.

In the 1990s, as an Olympic sport with megabuck TV contracts, international judo had to change its look. For spectators that didn't know a lot about judo, it was confusing to watch a match in which the score remained tied even though one contestant knocked his opponent down five times. Or worse yet, it was confusing to watch an overtime situation during a match in which the two combatants seemed to be out for a Sunday waltz with each other. Judo matches now have a time limit of five minutes for men and four minutes for women. Everything that happens within that specified time period counts toward deciding a winner when the buzzer sounds. The fact that once person attacked more effectively than the other, even if no one was knocked off balance, counts as a *kinsa* or edge. Thus, if a contestant is knocked onto his buttocks, his opponent receives a koka.

So why is this important? Well, some techniques that seem easier to execute on an unwary opponent are less likely to get an ippon or wazari. Thus, you can win if you're fair defensively. Many a World or Olympic championship has been won on a well-protected koka lead. Perhaps we should, as judo coach John Ross pointed out, "Practice koka techniques."

Tosh Seino (bottom), executing an unknown throw on Yuzo Koga.

Photo courtesy of Judo Journal

Yasuhiro Yamashita (left) is shown attempting to throw Hitoshi Saito.
Both *judoka* won gold medals at the 1984 Olympics.

ENDORPHINS

Runners after a time experience a "runner's high," which happens when endorphins (natural opiates) are released in the body. They feel euphoric and energized, and feel they can run forever and faster. Nothing can stop them. It seems that all is right in the universe.

Not every runner will experience this, nor will they experience it each time they run. Some may experience it somewhat yet will still enjoy it. Perhaps this is why runners get addicted to running.

There are also highs like this in judo, but most *judoka* are so busy at war with their opponents that they're unable to relish them. Since things change quickly during a match, judoka are anxious to go on to the next crucial situation. While during a match you seemingly don't get a "high" when you throw your opponent, you are probably experiencing chemical changes and endorphin releases in your body that prod you to keep attempting to throw him.

The problem is that most judoka don't celebrate overcoming adversity in their matches often enough. Usually, they don't reminisce about a job well done until way after the match is over. Immediately after a throw, you should probably emphasize, at least inwardly, the fact that you were able to throw your opponent and that you had complete control over him or her. Now take note, ask yourself, "How do I really feel?"

Look to the endorphins in judo.

Before Roger Bannister, no one believed anyone could run a mile in under four minutes. Before Nadia Comaneci, who believed a gymnast could get a string of tens? Yet even these records are being broken in the 2000s. If the modern Olympics have been around since 1904, why are these records being broken in the 2000s? Why haven't they been broken earlier? Are men and women changing? Have training, equipment and coaching methods altered performance? If they have evolved, what led to this new plateau?

It's spelled B E L I E F—a belief that it can be done, that a limitation is merely a hurdle to be overcome. It's the mind telling the body it's OK to succeed. It's the instant when the weight-lifter who is about to lift more than he has ever lifted before in his career, says to himself "I'm going to do it! I'm going to do it! I'm going to do it! I'm going to do it! I'm going to do it! Grrrrr! I did it!"

It may even extend beyond belief. It's knowing it has to be done and then doing it. But believing still has an element of uncertainty. It's like the old lady who picks up the car so her trapped son could escape death. Just do it! Stop disbelief! Don't think it can't be done.

Photo © Bob Willingham, 1998

How does a beautiful throw like this come to fruition? You picture it
in your mind, you practice it, you believe it and you do it!

Photo by Hayward Nishioka

Major players like Christoph Leininger (right) not only execute techniques but use the contest rules and competition area to their advantage.

Photo courtesy of Judo Journal

1995 World and 1996 Olympic champion Powel Nastula (left) is an expert in leg picks, lifts and one-handed judo.

10 THINGS FOR STAYING AHEAD OF THE GAME   2.22

If you want to be a successful *judoka* in the 1990s and beyond, here's what you need to do:

1. Be in exemplary cardiovascular condition.

2. Have a technique-oriented mind-set.

3. Be able to attack from any angle, anytime, with any technique.

4. Truncate the time of attack. In other words, as soon as you grip—attack!

5. Do one-handed judo.

6. Understand the rules and use them to your advantage.

7. Study gripping techniques, especially how to release your opponent's grip.

8. Make quick transitions from your standing techniques to your mat. The longer you wait to enter your mat techniques, the more difficult it will be to get them.

9. Be able to plan, execute and evaluate your progress in judo.

10. Be tenacious.

Dr. Jigoro Kano (1860-1938) at the young age of 22 founded judo. A sport that has come to be the second most participated sport in the world. First being soccer. Through its practice its participants hopefully enrich their lives by using the intrinsic principals of self-perfection, mutual welfare and benefit, and maximum efficiency with minimum effort.

Photo courtesy of Hayward Nishioka

When we say "I", do we really mean "I" alone? For example, "I' won the U.S. Championship. "I" beat him. "I'm" tough. "I" am the greatest. Or, does "I" also in part represent those people within our personal environment who have brought us to this point. We sometimes egotistically claim to be solely our own domain and give little thought of those, whose support was essential to "our" success. Nishioka wins in 1965 when Japanese Nationals were allowed to compete.

MY SUPPORT GROUP

My uncle Howard and my maternal grandmother introduced me to things Japanese. In Japan, she was a master of the lute. "Iemoto of Yoshida-ryu" Tomi Kumagai. She also taught koto, shamisen and the Chikuzen biwa (lute). She would practice till the strings of the instruments would draw blood from her fingertips.

Photo courtesy of Hayward Nishioka

Photo courtesy of Hayward Nishioka

ne thinks they become champions by themselves. Maybe some do, but for the most part they are with the help of family and friends whose adulation, encouragement and financial support play an l part of making it to the top! This is my support system. This is my family.

Photo courtesy of Roy Murakami

Judo was first introduced to the world at the 1932 Olympics in Los Angeles. Where Dr. Kano gave a demonstration and a lecture. Standing with him are many of the leaders of early judo in Los Angeles who never envisioned that it would be more than a cultural sport, "but," Kano did. I was fortunate to have met many many of these early leaders who kept the flames of judo alive for us. Senseis Hagio, Nagano, Yamanouchi, Yamada, and of course Seigo Murakami, head instructor at the Manzanar relocation camp pictured below. Above Dr. Kano stands 8th man in from the left.

Photo courtesy of Roy Murakami

Manzanar - a great dojo with great leaders and great students.

Photo courtesy of Roy Murakami

The products of Manzanars Judo Dojo spread throughout the United States. Among them Shigeo Tashima, the Tamura brothers, Toru Takamatsu, Kenji Yamada, Oshima, Hank Okamura, Dick Fukuyama and many more.

Risei Kano and his (entourage?) interspersed with leaders from the Northern California (during the 1960s).

The intensity and effort of getting to the top is shown in the throw as well as the defense.

Photo courtesy of Hayward Nishioka

The Winning Team at the 1965 National Championships in San Francisco. Southern California Judo Leaders in suits [back, L-R]: Frank Emi, Dan Oka, ?, Clyde Davina, Shag Okada, Shegeo Tashima, Toshiro Daigo (All-American Champion), Matoba, Matsubara, Asano, Mas Yoshida; [middle L-R]: Kenneth Kuniyuki, Kikuchi, Seigo Murakami, Mat Van Levwyn, Kiro Nagano, Shegeo Tashima, Risei Kario (Son of Jigoro Kano), Richard Fukuwa, Renzo Shibata, Harry Fukuwa, Bob Jarvis; [front L-R]: Kenso Kiyohiro, Hayward Nishioka, Toshiyuki Seino, Clyde Davina, Tatsuro Itani, Seino, Isao Mura and Kinjo.

East Coast 1960s.
East Coast: Faces from the past tell a tale of
dedication without a single word uttered. Who
do you see and what do you know about them?
Many faces, many stories.

Photo courtesy of Hayward Nishioka

H. Nishioka and brother Thomas with their step-father and very first judo instructor, Dan Oka. At that time, I never knew what a great man he was. Today some fathers can't even take care of their own children. He not only nurtured us, he loved us.

Photo courtesy of Hayward Nishioka

My second instructor, Ryusei Inoyue *(shichidan)* of sen shin *dojo* was the kind of man that Dr, Kano was proud of.

Nishioka with 3rd instructor
Kenneth Kuniyuki and the
Seinan Dojo team.

Photo courtesy of Hayward Nishioka

Photo courtesy of Hayward Nishioka

Porter (left) and Hayward Nishioka at the 1960 National Championships. Tampa, Florida. Phil Porter
enius. He introduced the concept of selling judo and did much to introduce judo to areas that we
have left untapped.

Photo courtesy of Hayward Nishioka

The Nanka Team
(Southern California
Judo Team) with the
winning National Team
Banner 1960.

Photo courtesy of Hayward Nishioka

Nishioka at
Sen Shin Dojo
1956.

1st instructor
Dan Oka
(step-father)

2nd instructor
Ryusei Inouy

The *uchimata* is one of the
more popular throws in contest
judo. The incomparable Tosh
Seino never wasted time;
he only wasted opponents.

Photo courtesy of Isao Wado

One of "Nanka" (Southern
California) judo team of
the 60's.

STARS OF THE 60's

HOKKA vs NANKA ALL STAR JUDO TOURNAMENT AT LOS ANGELES OCTOBER 2, 1960

In the 50's and 60's while judo was relatively unknown in many parts of the U.S., California enjoyed great team matches between Southern and Northern California.

Our first Olympic Judo Team; George Harris an African American, Jim Bregman a Jewish American, coach Yosh Uchida and Paul Maruyama Japanese Americans, and Senator Ben "Nighthorse" Campbell an American Indian.

1965 World Olympic Champion Isao Inokuma throwing Russias Anzer Kidnadze.

[L-R] Hayward Nishioka, Ben Campbell (US Senator, R. Party Colorado), George Gress, Richard Fukuwa and Mickey Tsuchida. U.S. judo team to Europe in the mid 60's.

Harvard Univ. graduate Dr. Bill Paul, a 1964 Olympic alternate executing a *haraigoshi*.

Photo courtesy of Hayward Nishioka

"Unbelievable." That is until you experienced Bruce Lee, who really was more incredible off the screen than on it.

Photo courtesy of Hayward Nishioka

Hayward Nishioka with good friends Igor Zatsepin (middle) and Gene LeBell.

Bob Wall, karate champion, actor, businessman and friend.

Photo courtesy of Hayward Nishioka

Jitta (6th dan) at 71 years of age. Still
Would not back down from a challenge.
heart he will always be *judoka*.

LACC Alumnus Women's U.S. judo
great Diane Tudela executing her
famous arm bar.

Photo courtesy of Diane Tudela

Nishioka with friend Dan Alef, chief
instructor at Santa Inez, CA Judo club.

[L-R] Yosh Uchida, President of U.S.A. Judo Senior I.J.F. "A" Referee George Uchida and Executive Director Bill Rosengerg

Photo courtesy of Hayward Nishioka

One of America's great Judo leaders, Frank Fullerton set the tone for organizational progress for 16 years as its president. Currently he is the sport director for the Pan American Judo Union.

Photo courtesy of Hayward Nishioka

Former U.S. Judo Grand Champion and Olympian George Harris, with [L-R] Susan Oles and Women's Judo pioneer and Organizer "Rusty" Kanokogi. She was responsible for the first World Women's Judo Championships, and was a major factor in getting women's judo accepted into the Olympics.

Photo courtesy of Hayward Nishioka

Two Unsung heroes: Shag Okada (7th dan) who, in spite of tough post-war times as a Japanese-America sings the National anthem with pride. He produced two Olympians. Leon Garrie was the architect for California Judo Inc. and its first vice-president. Often ahead of his time and thus misunderstood. His th unpopular decisions have over time been found to have been sound ones. He was both mentor and frie

Photo courtesy of Hayward Nishioka

ongest serving officer of
;A Judo, Verna Larking.

Dr. David Matsumoto, one of the 'movers and shakers' for U.S. Judo. Currently, he is the Director of Development. His other job, however, is that of being a professor in the psychology department at San Francisco State University.

Photo courtesy of Hayward Nishioka

Professor Michel Brousse of the University of Bordeaux, France. Author and soul mate from the other side of the world.

Photo courtesy of Michel Brousse

ird Nishioka standing with Y.S.
President of the International
Association.

Photo courtesy of Hayward Nishioka

Bob Brink, former President of the U.S.J.F., brought in a profesional touch to judo.

Photo courtesy of Hayward Nishioka

Francois Besson Sports Director of the International Judo Federation

Nishioka with USJF President Mitchel Palacio.

Photo courtesy of Hayward Nishioka

1992 Olympic silver medalist Jason Morris (left) pictured with Olympian Steve Cohen, head coach of the U.S. Olympic Judo team for the "2000 games" in Australia.

Photo courtesy of Hayward Nishioka

Gokor Chivichyan—a superfight winner at the 1997 World Fight Federation and head instructor of Hiyastan Judo Club — was the captain of Los Angeles City College's judo club in the late

Coach Gene LeBell (Hachidan) with Mickey Crouch (Shodan), the owner of the Haunted House Discotheque. The only one on Hollywood Blvd. that had a *dojo* in it. It was called the Welcome Mat dojo, which in 1969 won the Southern California Team Judo Championship.

Photo courtesy of Hayward Nishioka

One of my first coaching assignments was for Nanka Yudanshakai 1977.

LONG BEACH STATE UNIVERSITY JUDO TEAM

Photo courtesy of Michael Hart

Students at California State University at Long Beach, Judo Club.

Photo courtesy of Michael Hart

Photo courtesy of Michael Hart

[L-R] Michael Hart, Bill Cabrera and Hayward Nishioka.

A classic shot of the titans of the '60s and '70s middleweight division. Any one of them on a given day could have fought up two weight divisions and still have won. [L-R] Hayward Nishioka, Rene Zeelinberg, Pat Burris, Tom Masterson and Paul Muruyama.

Catching shots like this incredible throw requires skill and a lot of luck. But... on a videotape it gets a lot easier. With video you get to see the whole action and not just a snapshot. You can also play it over and over even in slow motion, you get to scrutinize every motion, and when your student says "I don't do that!" you say "Look here!"

TITANS AND VIDEO CREW

Photo courtesy of Joe Serianni

The Killer "B's" a group of International "B" referees who became "A's" because they critiqued each other. Sometimes harshly, but always as friends. Standing from L-R are: Russel Scherer, Fletcher Thornton, Martin Bregman, Hayward Nishioka, Mr. and Mrs. Frank Morales and Tom Seabasty. Missing from the picture are Mel Applebaum and Rick Celotto.

Photo courtesy of Utako Hashima

The video crew for U.S.A. Judo: Low Dong, George Stanich, Hayward Nishioka, Young Park and organizer "Utako" Hashima at the 1995 World Championships, Japan.

Photo courtesy of Jason Morris

The "Dynamic Duo"—Jimmy Pedro, world judo champion and 1996 Olympic bronze medalist and Jason Morris, 1992 Olympic silver medalist— terrorized the rest of the judo world during the '90s. They're considered to be the finest judoka in the world.

Photo courtesy of Kelly Barnes

Double duty champion Ulla Werbrouck (right) of Belgium ('95 World and '96 Olympic champion) with Kelly Barnes U.S. elite player.

History maker Mike Swain made history in Essen, Germany in 1987 as he became America's first male world's champion. He also made history as he brought to T.V., "PRO-JUDO."

Photo courtesy of Hayward Nishioka

Photo courtesy of Kelly Barnes

Hayward Nishioka with Bruce Lee and Chuck Norris. Photo courtesy Oliver Pang.

COACHING

U.S. coaching staff members Evilio Garcia and Hayward Nishioka standing with All-Japan champions Sumio Endo and Yoshinori Takenchi, IJF referee Joon Chi, U.S. Manager Jim Colgan and Professor Matsumura.

Photo courtesy of Joon Chi

Photo courtesy of Joon Chi

[Above] Pan American and World team coaching staff David Matsumoto, Yoichiro Matsumara, Joon Chi, Lou Moyerman, Steve Cohen, Steve Isono, Evilio Garcia, Jim Colgan, Hayward Nishioka and Ed Liddie.

President of the I.J.F., Y.S. Park in the shadows as Jim Kojima Director of Referees for the I.J.F., scans the reception room. In the foreground International referees James Colgan, Mel Applebaum and Hayward Nishioka await dinner.

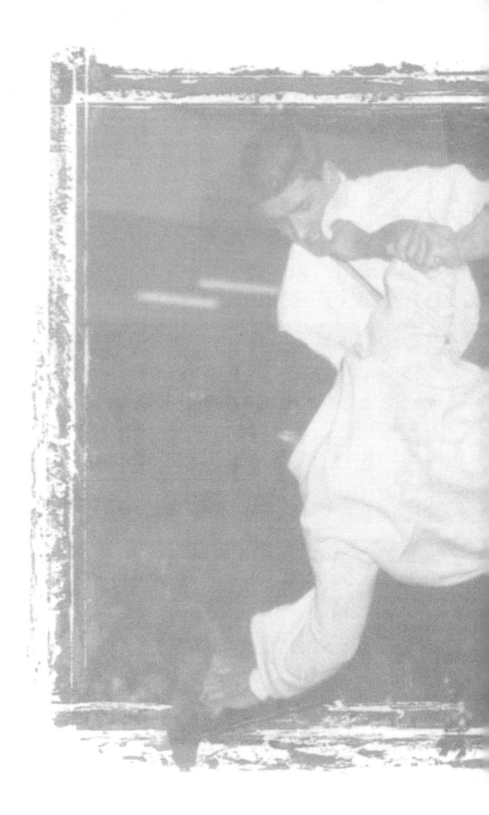

CHAPTER 3
STRATEGIC

"SEN RYAKU"

Legendary 17th-century swordsman Miyamoto Musashi once had to deal with multiple opponents. While viewing his surroundings, he noticed a nearby rice field. In rice fields, a lot of water is boxed in by upraised walkways. These walkways allow farmers to contain the water and maneuver quickly from area to area.

After killing the head of the clan that was pursuing him, Musashi ran quickly toward the rice field and down one of the pathways. In close pursuit were members of the clan, who had hoped to destroy him. Unfortunately, those who opted to slosh through the rice field gave up their mobility and were destroyed in turn. Those who attacked on the pathway were forced to attack single file, and they were slaughtered as well.

In competitive judo, all the avenues of strategy as they pertain to the competition area have yet to be explored. In most matches, attention is given to engaging an opponent toe-to-toe. Perhaps someday there will be more matches resembling a chase scene, in which your opponent is led into the danger zone, all the while mindful of you. He may be led to believe several things:

1. You are pressured, and you are retreating.

2. He will force you out of bounds and gain a score.

3. He's going to get you to stay in the red danger zone for 5 seconds and be penalized.

Another advantageous use of the competition area is the corners. If you can force your opponent into a corner, press his strong side to the boundary line and face so that his only option is to move to your favorite side, and catch him. You may be able to devise strategies against your opponent's strengths and weaknesses. If your opponent is weak on the mat, for example, take him to the mat as often as you can. Or if you are weak on the mat, fight your battles standing up and as close to the edge as possible so you can wiggle your way out of bounds. If necessary, find and attack the opponents weak points.

Strategy may not even be confined to the engagement itself, but could be found in the preparation phase when you can customize your judo to suit the demands of certain competitors who always seem to try to occupy the top spot.

Like Miyamoto Musashi, we must be aware of our environment and utilize it to our advantage.

Photo by Hayward Nishioka

The person being thrown relaxed because he thought he was going to be thrown out of bounds. The thrower will win the match as long as his foot remains inside the boundary line, even though he threw his opponent out of bounds. Players tend to relax near the edge of the competition area. This is a big mistake for the opponent and a strategic coup for you.

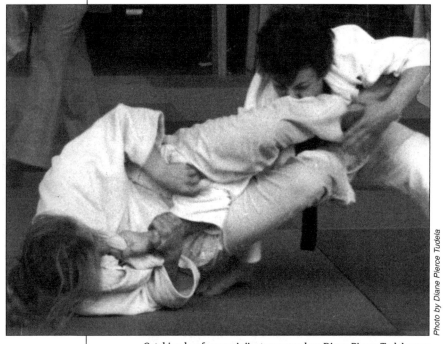

Catching her famous jujigatame-arm bar, Diane Pierce-Tudela was able to win nine national titles. She was also the co-captain for the L.A. City College Judo team from 1979-1980.

INCREASING YOUR CHANCES   3.2

The window of success is open for only a short time. You must seize the moment or it will be lost forever. Judo competitors usually peak when they are around 25 or 30 years old. Some peak sooner, some peak later. Judo, by nature, is demanding physically, neurologically and psychologically. Sustaining top-level conditioning for extended periods of time is difficult.

There are few who make it to the Olympic games in judo who are older than their mid-30s. So if we counted backward from age 35 by increments of four years (since the Olympics are held every four years), a 35-year-old person could have been in the Olympics at age 35, 31, 27, 23, 19 and 16—six times. During these years, unless you're independently wealthy or unusually healthy and lucky, you'll have to make sacrifices in the following areas: education, social life, marriage, sweethearts, kids, job opportunities, advancements, material things, health, timing and luck.

Each year that you waste beyond age 25 reduces the likelihood that you will make the Olympic team. The costs and pressures increase; you want to get married and start a family, you want to make money and own a house, a good car, etc.; your injuries heal slower; your muscles and nerves heal even more slowly; and your physical abilities are at their peak, but they will soon decline. What should you do?

Fight as if your life depended on the match. Fight as if you will never get another chance if you lose this one. Fight, fight, fight!

"When in doubt, fight!"—Ulysses S. Grant

Sometimes you get only one chance to attend a State Championship, a National Championship, an International Championship, a World Championship or the Olympics. When you're there you're overawed by the magnitude of the event—the pomp and ceremony, the different people, different nations, colors and flags—and wonder, "What am I doing here? Do I even belong here?"

The answer is yes. You—not the ones who stayed home—qualified. You had the guts, the backing, even the luck. You are the one who's there. You are the qualified representative. Your opponents are not any better than the sum of their previous practice sessions. Many times, the difference between a winner and a loser is that the winner said to himself, "I belong here, that gold medal belongs to me, and I'm going to fight you and show you. How dare you even get out on the same mat with me? I'll bury you now. This is my turf. This is my home." Now repeat the words, "I belong here,, that gold medal belongs to me, and I'm going to fight you and show you. How dare you even get on the same mat as me?. I'll bury you, this is my turf, this is my home!"

Photo by Christine Penick Lincoln

Pictured here are (from left to right) Lynn Roethke, Liliko Ogasawara, Kathleen Dalton and Christy Springer. Ogasawara and Roethke both made themselves at home by being silver medalists in separate World Championships (Roethke in 1987 and Ogasawara in 1993).

Photo courtesy of Rene Zeelinberg

U.S. judo champion Rene Zeelinberg (with head bowed) continues his fearful grimace as he upends his opponent with a *haraigoshi* (hip sweep).

HOW YOU LOOK IS HOW YOU FEEL 3.4

A relaxed body exhibits a relaxed mind. What is the face of fear or terror? Can you picture it? Can you feel it? What is the face of anger? Do your jaws clench and your eyes narrow? What is the face of sorrow? Does your mouth droop at the corners? Does your head drop forward? Do your shoulders slump forward? Can you feel happiness and rage at the same time? What is the face of anguish and joy? Have you seen the face of a person having these juxtaposed feelings? Or do you switch from one face to the other in an instant, depending on which is the more dominant emotion? Can you hold and control one emotion over another for an extended period of time? Does it take energy to do this? What would be the benefit?

As you may have guessed, the idea is to concentrate on one emotion to the exclusion of another. In this manner, you won't want to waste precious energy fighting yourself. Too many times, fighters step on the mat with a sad, kicked-in-the-side puppy-dog look, or a look of fear and worry. Now, you're fighting yourself with energy better spent on one thought: aggression.

In addition, your opponent may be reading you. And if he's reading you correctly and has you in a corner on the run, he's going to go for the kill.

Such are American ethics, as one of my professors, Dr. Frank, used to say: "When you've got a man down, stomp on him. If you don't believe me, look at Nixon." So even when you're down, don't show it. Don't act it. Don't be it.

From time to time, you should take a mental inventory of what you have and what you have to do. It's the "what you have to do" that is important. You should review your matches mentally by thinking about your opponent's strengths and weaknesses, practicing avoiding and attacking, and readying yourself for your real match. If you fought your opponent before, you should almost feel the impending attack and almost twitch in defense.

You may also include losses in these mental inventories. In these cases, you should review in your mind how you lost the match so you can prevent it from happening again. Conversely, if you won the match you should reflect on how it felt to win and determine ways to remain a winner. You may, however, want to try another technique the next time you fight the opponent you defeated, since he'll probably be waiting for you and will try to counter your winning technique.

During this mental review, remember to be cautious of your opponent's favorite throws and how he telegraphs them. Tighten up the loose ends. Dig deep into your soul and will yourself not to fall for his techniques or his style.

These mental inventories have to be emotional bouts. They can occur while standing in a line, driving your car on a long trip, or even before dozing off to sleep. Almost all serious players take a mental inventory. Don't you think so?

Anton Geesink (top) is shown throwing Akio Kaminaga at the World Judo Championships in Paris in December 1961. Geesink would win the championships that year, becoming the first-ever non-Japanese *judoka* to do so. Geesink later defeated Kaminaga again at the 1964 Olympics to become the first-ever non-Japanese competitor to win an Olympic gold medal in judo.

Wilhelm Ruska (top) won a gold medal in two judo divisions (open and heavyweight) at the 1972 Olympics in Munich, Germany. This feat can no longer be duplicated since there is no longer an open weight division in judo at the Olympics.

THE ADVANTAGE GOES TO THE CHAMPION   3.6

Champions know what it feels like to be champions. Others never think about it. Champions have a confidence that non-champions don't have. Champions know they have to remain champions by winning championships. They have a different energy level.

Champions also expect more out of themselves. Once you taste success, you become a different person. This success reflects in your demeanor, and others interact differently with you. You definitely have the edge.

Officials also seem to favor champions. A challenger, in order to win, must soundly defeat the champion. If the challenger is unknown, he is at even more of a disadvantage. The champion's ego and reputation are on the line. The referee may know who Yasuhiro Yamashita or Peter Seizenbacher is, but who is Frank Ness? The advantage always goes to the champion.

During competitions, we often get apprehensive and fight a war instead of a battle and a battle instead of an individual. Novices get overwhelmed at tournaments because they see so many competitors at one time. This, in addition to the excitement of a tournament site, gives them the illusion that they must face everyone in their weight division on their way to the championship. In actuality, according to U.S. International Coach Jim Herbek, there are usually only five to six rounds to the final match.

In addition, novices tend to fight their second and third battles before they even arrive at the tournament site. They might think, "I don't know who my next opponent is, but Olympic champion Yasuhiro Yamashita is in my pool." Now they're fighting Yamashita before they even face their next opponent. Perhaps Saito and Rashwan are also in their pool. It's emotionally draining, isn't it?

"This is your next opponent!" Yasuhiro Yamashita (left) is
executing a left *osotogari* (outside reap).

Referee James Takemori watches as Bill Paul (standing on one leg)
sends his opponent flying with a left *haraigoshi* (hip sweep).

While it is a good idea for you to have some idea who is
in your pool, you must be able to zone in on your very
next opponent or else you will constantly be fighting three
or four battles at a time before you begin your next
match. This could be disastrous, emotionally and physically. Besides, the worst scenario is that you will worry,
get an ulcer and lose in the first round to your unknown
opponent. This is all part of the mental discipline of judo,
which is "Zone in, and fight one opponent at a time."

Isao Wada, head instructor at Gardena Judo Club, executing his famous *osotogari* (outside major trap). When you get smashed like this, you really know that losing is like dying. If Wada's opponent landed on cement...ouch! Well, you know what I mean!

LOSING IS LIKE DYING   3.8

You can practice your judo like it was a game, or you can take it to a higher plane. If it's just a game, you don't mind losing; it's just a game. If you take it to a higher plane, you are mindful that judo is a derivative of *jujitsu*. In turn, *jujitsu* is a derivative of the arts of warfare. The ancient Japanese designed *jujitsu* techniques to control, maim or kill others. In the new millennium, judo is a refined Olympic sport with rules that facilitate competition and safety. Nevertheless, serious *judoka* instinctively know that losing is like dying.

With competitors armed with this mind-set, the upcoming match becomes a cut above a mere game. Now it's a struggle between life and death. Now your bloodstream carries more than just oxygen. Your pace is quicker, your heart beats faster and stronger, you can't catch your breath, and your perspiration leaks from every pore of your skin even as you sit quietly trying to contemplate the upcoming battle. Many competitors will actually suffer a sick feeling of impending doom. Others will throw up. Others will freeze up. Some will give up. Still others will clumsily stumble their way through a match for which they were insufficiently prepared.

For those who have come prepared to do battle, there is a certain serenity that occurs upon the grasping of your opponent's judo *gi*. The shouts of the coaches and the crowd are but a murmur. While the match is going on, everything is moving fast and slow at the same time. Openings in your opponent's defense are met with an automatic response. Your body moves before your brain reflects. There is no time to reflect on the possible outcome. You have already equated each possible knockdown as an injury. A loss would surely mean that you're dead. Even so, you are resigned to the battle at hand. Now is the time to solve the equation of life and death.

Are your hands sweating? Are you feeling flush or sick to your stomach? Are you worried about the outcome of an upcoming match? What are you going to do?

Nervousness can be a positive experience. It is usually a result of your mind telling your body to release epinephrine and get ready to do battle. But someone can also be so nervous that he freezes up and cannot function correctly. The trick is to not be so nervous that you freeze up, but not be so complacent that you don't get your adrenaline flowing.

Some competitors get so nervous that they throw up or become ill due to all the stress. Two stories come to mind that explain how to gauge and contend with nervousness.

This first story is somewhat off-color. Shibayama, a *sensei* at the Kodokan, would often relate how he would gauge if he was ready for a *shiai*. When his scrotum felt shriveled and tight he would do poorly, and when his scrotum hung loose he seemed to do well. While there may not be a scientific answer to this phenomenon, it should provide some comic relief as you test out the hypothesis (provided you've got the equipment). As they say in Hawaii, "Hang loose."

Another way to contend with that ill feeling is to direct your attention across the mat prior to the match, and stare at your opponent. Picture yourself defeating him. After all, he is the one to blame. If it wasn't for him, you wouldn't be feeling this nervous or ill. It is all his fault! How dare he challenge you this way. Get mad now! Hate him for being there. Pretend he's done awful things to your family. Then kick his ---.

As a retired competitor, I can tell you from experience that you will actually miss that awful feeling of death in the air before a match, because it reminds you of how alive you really are. There are few exhilarating moments in life as those in which the outcome is decided by the intensity of two opposing bodies fighting for existence.

So go ahead and immerse yourself in nervousness. Sweat it out with the rest of us. We're nervous only because we have to wait so long for the answer, an answer we get only from the actual match itself. So don't worry so much that you freeze up. The answer will always be there at the end of the match.

One nervous, one calm.

Being thrown during a match or losing is the *judoka's* greatest fear.
It's funny. Most judoka don't worry about getting injured or killed
during a match. That's because in judo, everyone gets up off the mat
and fights again.

FEAR

Excessive fear is a detriment to progress. Some *judoka* are in a constant state of fear of losing a practice session, a match or a tournament; of entering tournaments or fighting a certain competitor; or of injuries, what others might think or say, losing face, death or even entering into a throw.

We probably never overcome our fear; we only learn to better cope with it. The kamikaze pilots of World War II, who put their fears aside for a greater cause, suddenly become very powerful. Think about what it would be like to have such an adversary—one whose sole purpose was to defeat you, and who didn't care whether he lived or died in the process. Although you kept knocking him down, he would arise and attack you again and again like a machine. This would certainly be a fearful situation.

Now, let's turn this concept of fear around a bit. Isn't it reasonable to assume that if you are subject to fear, your opponent—given the right frame of mind—may also experience fear? Thus, your frame of mind would be, "I'm going to fight him with everything I've got, even if it kills me." To be totally committed...now, that's fearsome.

The alternative is to freeze with fear and be cut down and returned to the void without even as much as an epitaph to commemorate your visit to Earth.

One of the most courageous sports is basketball. No matter if the score is 100-110 with only one minute to go, the team down by 10 keeps going. Even if they have no chance of winning, they continue to fight on.

They do it because there is always a chance, however small, of reversing the odds. They do it because the coach wants to see what the team is made of. They do it because if they do anything less they'll never really know what the true outcome is and won't know what to work on to improve. They do it to cut their losses.

Judoka could learn a lesson from basketball players. Many judoka who lose a chance to take first place will lose hope and will not try their best to continue fighting as hard as possible. Who wants second or third place? Who wants to be in a picture on the victory stand in second place with people you have defeated before? Who wants to continue on when there is no hope of winning first place? But what if it means an Olympic medal? A World Championship medal? A National Championship medal? A State Championship medal? A local medal? A *dojo* medal? At what point might you not want to be in that picture? And what about the idea of cutting your losses?

Illustration by Heyward Nishioka

Don't give up, don't ever give up!
Even if the game is over, don't give up.

Photo by Hayward Nishioka

1992 Olympic judo silver medalist Jason Morris (right), one of America's most talented *judoka*, usually disposed of his opponents quickly.

WEAKER OPPONENTS   3.12

The weaker the opponent, the quicker you should elimi-
nate him. If you can throw him in two seconds, do it! You
will have more important opponents to fight during the
day. The less your weaker opponent knows about your
rhythm and style, the more easily you can dispose of him.
The more time you spend with him, the more he'll be able
to overcome you.

"I was trying to warm up with him, but got worn out
instead," is the lament a coach does not want to hear. If
the stakes are high, you don't have time to spend warming up on the mat during a match. The day will be long
enough, and your energies can be better spent on those
who deserve it.

During a tournament, you will have an average of five to
seven matches that could go the distance. That's at least
25 minutes in which you will have to tax your energy
store. You might as well spend less time against the
weaker opponents in the earlier rounds, and save the
best for last.

The Japanese saying *"Yudan tai Teki"* may apply here. It
means "Letting your guard down is your biggest enemy."
If you let your guard down against weaker opponents,
they may catch you off-guard and defeat you. Don't take
chances, especially against weaker opponents.

The tougher your opponent, the more time you want to spend with him. If you just go out and go over, you obviously have no chance to defeat him at all.

The longer the match, the more you will learn about your opponent. You might not be able to defeat him this time, but you may be able to do so in the future. If you've been out on the mat with your opponent for a while, you'll have some experiences with him to reflect on and to find faults in his defense.

Following are some suggestions to help you prolong your match:

1. Fight grips
When grip fighting, try to get the most advantageous grip while leaving your opponent feeling uncomfortable with his own. This position usually leaves you ready to initiate an attack. If your opponent has his grip, you should attempt to break free as quickly as possible. If this is done properly, it can look as though both of you are unwilling to take a grip.

2. Don't tie up right away
The average judo match is four to five minutes in length. You'll have plenty of time, so you needn't rush into the affray. Take your time and be especially wary at the beginning of a grip or regrip, since a modern player can attack off the grip. This is even more evident in matches between lightweights. Heavyweights, as a rule, take their time.

3. Cross grips
In cross gripping, your right hand crosses over and grabs your opponent's right lapel, or vice versa. Your opponent will have difficulty attacking you through it. But be careful not to place both hands on the same side of your opponent's judo *gi* for more than five seconds or so without attacking. This action could be interpreted as a defensive attitude and can be penalized accordingly.

By judiciously applying these grips, you can buy time to see what makes your opponent tick. In some instances, cross gripping can bring added stress into the match as penalties can be given for non-combativity (hopefully for both of you, because this keeps the score even).

4. Attack a lot—especially near the edge—and float out, but be careful of false attack penalties.
Between grip fights, attack near the edge of the mat. Opponents sometimes let up near the edge, enabling you to catch them. Even if you don't catch your opponent and then float outside, you can't be penalized for stepping out of bounds. Furthermore, if between grip fighting you are attacking and your opponent is not attacking, your opponent might be given a non-combativity penalty. Hopefully, it will be his fourth one—*hansokumake*, loss by penalty.

5. If you're good on the mat, fight on the mat.
In tennis, if your opponent has a good forehand you try to hit more to his backhand. It is no different in judo. If your opponent is a better stand-up fighter, then take him to the mat. You might have a better chance of winning the match. Most *judoka* seem to prefer standing judo; therefore, your chances are better if you're halfway decent on the mat. Besides, mat work uses up time.

In this type of strategy, you have to be more afraid of getting defeated right away than being penalized to death. The name of the game is to increase your experience on the mat.

Photo by Hayward Nishioka

A U.S. champion vs. a U.S. champion. Toughing out the contest are Johnny Hobales (left) and Marcus Dawson (right).

There are no weight divisions at the All-Japan Championships, so you fight whomever you draw. This has made for some interesting matches through the years. In the late 1960s, Isao Okano—a light-middleweight—defeated all his heavyweight opponents to twice win the All-Japan Championships. In the 1990 All-Japan Championships, T. Koga and openweight champion Naoya Ogawa fought in the finals.

In all his previous matches, Koga defeated opponents who weighed over 95 kilograms (about 209 pounds). Now, the pressure was on. For Koga, who weighed roughly 71 kilograms (about 156 pounds), was going against the toughest of the heavyweights—World Champion Naoya Ogawa—and was giving up more than 50 pounds and a longer reach. Ogawa, on his part, was not going to have a walk in the park. Besides, what if he were to lose the All-Japan Championships to a shrimp? He'd be the laughingstock of judo history.

What should the big man do? What should the small man do?

For the small man, his advantage is movement. For the big man, his advantage is power. For the small man, it's cunning; for the big man, it's overbearing. The small man must make the big man move. The big man must anchor the target for an attack. The small man must do quick combinations with foot techniques. The big man must bury his opponent with a big technique. The small man must hit and run and make the match last. The big man must power the small man over and not give him a chance to embarrass him.

Ideally, the big man should learn to look like an elephant yet move like a cheetah. The small man should energize himself to feel heavy like an elephant yet attack like an unfed, wounded feline.

The match lasted more than four minutes. Koga was slightly in the lead. Ogawa, suddenly sensing a weakness, applied a *haraigoshi* (hip sweep) and powered Koga over. *Ippon!* But you could see the muscles relax in Ogawa's worried face. Had the match gone the distance, fate might have had a different outcome in store.

Heavyweight champion Alan Coage, a.k.a. Bad News Brown (left), in a grand championship match with Hayward Nishioka at the 1970 National Championships in Los Angeles, CA.

Photo by Hayward Nishioka

Mike Pachina (left), looking for a good grip.

GRIP FIGHTING

In judo competitions in the 2000s, *judoka* have to be able to do "grip and go judo." This means the ability to attack as a grip is taken. Japan's Ryako Tamura demonstrates perhaps the prime example of "grip and go judo." She throws many unwary opponents with *osotogari*, (outside major reaps) *kosotogari* (inside minor reaps) or *taiotoshi* (body drops) just as she grips her opponent's lapel, sometimes with only one hand.

You can claim dominance in a match from the first grip. Your goal should be to first get the grip that is most comfortable for you, then maintain it and attack. This is important, since in most cases the advantage in a match goes to the one who has the grip first.

The grip should be used as a preparatory step for an entry, not just as a means of stalling a match (unless you can convincingly manage it, and if you're ahead).

If you are right-handed, your right hand is the gauging hand. You can usually tell when your hand is bent correctly and is in the correct position to enter into a throw. The left hand is the pulling hand. When grip-fighting, the one who has pulled the other's arm out straighter than his own has the advantage.

An elaborate array of grips exist that may afford you some advantage during a match. Try them out. Most often when you feel comfortable, you are frustrating your opponent (which is something all good judoka like to do).

When some students begin judo training, they show promise as future Olympic champions. They're big, fast, strong and athletic. Yet as time goes on they practice less and less, until pretty soon they quit training altogether. Then there are those who, from the moment they stumble into the *dojo,* others look at them and say to themselves "Oh no!" Everyone uses them as practice dummies. And sometimes it's hard to tell where the mat begins and the human ends. But they stick it out and, lo and behold, become champions one day.

Some *judoka* are tough while working out at the dojo and can beat the best fighters. But when they enter a tournament, somehow they lose it. Conversely, there are those who get beaten by practically everyone but the kids in the class during practice; yet at a tournament, when the chips are down and it's time to play, something happens to them and they shine.

Some judoka seem invincible, and some seem destined to be perennial victims. Despite this, God is a comedian and will sometimes hand the keys of success to the victim, who will defeat the invincible. Remember the ugly duckling, David and Goliath, and Jack and the Beanstalk? So place your bets. Who is the eventual winner and the perennial loser? Anything is possible.

Gene Mauro (right), trying to defend and upend the heavier 300-pound Johnny Watts.

Photo by Hayward Nishioka

Two U.S. talents: Grace Jivaden (left) and Tonnie Barnes (right).

NIGATE

Awkward opponents will invariably cross your path. Many beginners and even some advanced *judoka* will be discouraged by certain opponents with whom they constantly have difficulty. They're called *nigate*.

It's funny, but at times these nigate may not even be very skilled or very strong. In fact, other players whom you will easily defeat will be able to throw them with ease. Yet you will have a hard time with them. It is really a matter of conflicting styles.

It's important to study why you have difficulty with this opponent. Is he left-handed? Does he use a cross grip, have disconnected movements or move in an opposite direction when you need to execute your throw? There is a myriad of possibilities. But by studying the reasons why you can't throw or defeat this opponent, you will become a wiser, better judoka.

The main thing is to not let these awkward opponents discourage you early in your training. Remember, even the best judoka in the world have their nigate to contend with.

Your opponent is tough. He's got a reputation as a clutch player—a come-from-behind, last-second guy. *Hajime!* Whoosh! You score the first point. Time goes on, there are only 30 seconds to go and no other points have been scored. Now he's pressing the attack.

Should I attack back? Should I go head-to-head? Should I just counter? Should I stall out the rest of the match and win by a *wazari?* What should I do? Hurry up! 30 seconds is an eternity. Think! Make a decision! Oh no, he's coming after me!

Photo by Christine Penick Lincoln

Doug Tono (right) is facing off with Jimmy Pedro at the Senior
National Championships in Florida. Pedro is ahead and Tono is pressing, as International referee E.K. Kawai oversees the match.

You don't really know how long a minute is until you have to fight your last minute in the finals of a major tournament with a tough nut while you're only a *koka* ahead.

How do you keep your lead without losing it? Well, naturally, don't make mistakes, specifically:

1. Stalling or non-combativity. This is a *shido* (slight infraction) penalty. But a shido and a koka carry equal weight. Oh, oh! Decision time.

2. False attacks. To avoid receiving a non-combativity penalty, some *judoka* fake an entry into a throw. If this move is apparent to the judges, it receives a shido penalty. If you're going to enter into a false attack, at least try to drag your opponent down to the ground because it looks better. At least it looks like a sincere attempt. Maybe, just maybe, the referee won't penalize you then.

3. Attacking when you don't need to attack. If there is a minute left in the match and you're a *wazari* ahead, then stall. So what if you receive a shido or even a *chui* (moderate infringement)? A wazari is worth more.

4. Not using *newaza* (mat work) to eat time. If you're unsure of your newaza skills, it's time you started practicing them. Every major player is skilled at mat work, not just to pin, choke and armbar, but to eat time when he is ahead.

5. Not using the edges. Using the edges is important. Better players play to the inside and force their opponents to the edge. Why? Because if you get thrown it's usually better since your opponent will throw himself, as well as you, out of bounds, therefore nullifying the

throw. Unless your opponent is well-skilled psychologically, it's harder to execute a throw near the edge; some players can, however. If you fall to the mat, you can roll out easily if you're near the edge. If you're in the middle of the mat, forget it.

6. If nobody has the advantage, the last minute of the match is crucial in terms of getting in an attack that will stick in the referees' minds. The brain should flash "Get a *kinsa!* Get a kinsa!" Attack, attack, attack! (A "kinsa" is a near-scoring throw or pin.)

7. The Cuban model is to get ahead early in the match and wait to counter the opponent who is overextending himself trying to catch up. Then "Wango." Its countertime.

Photo by Hayward Nishioka

U.S. Champion Valery Lafon (top) was a master at staying ahead.

3.20   ALTERING THE PACE

The difference between lightweight and heavyweight fighters is a matter of pace. If you're a heavyweight, you usually rely on your power to overcome your adversary. If you're a lightweight, you rely on your speed.

The larger man up against a smaller man should slow the pace of the match as much as possible, whereas the lighter person should try to speed up the match. The lighter person's strategy is to increase the number of times his heavier opponent must readjust his weight so he could make attempts to catch his heavier opponent off-guard with foot techniques.

The larger fighter's biggest problem is his self-image of being an "ogre" who overpowers rather than "slicks" his opponent. Take this advice: Forget your self-image and smack your opponent with power if you can. Your self-image will be much worse if you lose to an opponent who is 60 to 70 pounds lighter than you are.

You may also try changing the pace from slow to fast, or vice versa, several times within your workout or match. At any rate, use whatever advantage you have to its fullest.

Suggestions for altering the pace:

1. Move faster or slower. Depending on whose ahead and how much time is left.

2. Don't tie up when things are moving too fast for you. Cut away, cross grip and go to the mat.

3. Press your opponent with attacks.

4. Drag your opponent around.

5. Take your time returning to the match at the "matte" or "wait" call.

6. Return quickly to the affray at the "matte" or "wait" call.

Photo © Bob Willingham, 1998

World and Olympic champion David Douillet (top) of France demonstrates that a heavyweight can be fast, have technique and be as cunning as a lightweight. In a short-lived final match against Ernesto Perez of Spain at the 1996 Olympics in Atlanta, Georgia, Douillet executes a quick, powerful *uchimata* (inner thigh throw) to snatch the gold medal from him.

U.S. National Champion Bill Sanford (left) is shown throwing with his famous *sode tsurikomi goshi* (hanging sleeve hip throw).

BEING PREPARED

Try running into a gymnasium or *dojo* seconds before your match is about to begin. Now compare the feeling with that of having been at matside two or three minutes before your match.

You will usually experience an uneasy, up-in-the-air feeling of unpreparedness. Being prepared means you're at matside ready to go. You should have mentally thrown your opponent a number of times already. As you walk to the starting line, you should be confident but not overconfident, aggressive but not overly aggressive, and cautious but not to a fault.

At the 1993 World Judo Championships, one contestant lamented: "The wait was long. I didn't know when I was going to compete, then suddenly the coach came up to me and said 'You're up in ten minutes.' I didn't even know who my opponent was! It was as if I was in the haze of a bad dream over which I had no control. It was all overwhelming and I lost."

Situations like these often occur because players are not prepared. When I think of someone who was prepared, I always think of U.S. Olympian and National Champion Steve Seck. He would constantly watch his opponents' matches and, from what he'd seen, make mental notes as to how to handle his opponents. If he had enough time, he would practice moves to defeat specific opponents. On the day of competition he was at matside, prepared to go. He had studied the draw sheets and knew who his opponents would be. He was prepared to be the winner.

"Giri giri no kimochi" means the feeling of the last moments or the moment of truth. You are pressed into a corner, and now it's time to act or die, or maybe both. Tsutomu Ohshima, a famous karate instructor, speaks often about this moment and says great results often come from it.

It can be, for example, a time like that split second before the snake lunges forward to take his prey; or the blink of an eye, when the mongoose counters to take on the cobra. It's the moment when time is short and you need to attack or lose.

During a four- or five-minute match, many *judoka* wait until the last minute to become aware of the "giri giri no kimochi" and crank up their engines and move.

Lightweight competitors, who fight for the full four to five minutes, are better aware of this feeling of being cornered. From the *"Hajime"* command, 1993 World Champion Ryoko Tamura, who weighs 48 kilograms, constantly attacks as if there were only 10 seconds left in the match. This cornered feeling has enabled her to defeat many opponents within the first 10 seconds of a match.

Yuzo Koga (on one leg) always fought with the *giri giri no kimochi.*

Attack as your opponent is about to attack. Beat him to the punch.

"SEN NO SEN"

"Sen" means "line" in Japanese. It's the line of attack. It's the feeling of weakness in your opponent's defense during which you attack. It's your entry. "Sen no sen" means "line of a line." Sometimes you can sense that your opponent is about to attack. You attack at that very instant, thereby taking away his line of attack; thus, "sen no sen."

Now figure out what "sen zen no sen" means.

Judo competitors today must be able to perform standing up as well as on the ground. Approximately 30 to 35 percent of international competition is won by mat techniques. Those not able to fight on the mat will fall prey to those who can.

A definite advantage to mat work is that points are attained as a matter of time or submission. Little is left to the official to decide. For example, a referee may call a throw a *yuko* (superior advantage) and one side judge may call it a *wazari,* while the other side judge may call it a *koka.* When the time is up a pin is an *ippon.* An armbar or choke is a submission or a broken arm or a choke. The referee's judgment does not enter into the scoring picture in mat work the same way as it does with a throw.

Another advantage to mat work is that it allows you to practice judo at a slower pace with less traumatic movements. This means that there is a lower rate of injury since movements can be better controlled. Thus, injured/recovering students can partake in practice sessions. Also, the older *judoka* who's lost the competitive edge yet wants to practice judo for exercise can do so with a greater peace of mind, knowing that he'll be able to make it to work the next day, injury-free.

Photo by Hayward Nishioka

If you're looking at the lights in the ceiling, you're in the wrong position on the mat.

Photo by Christine Penick Lincoln

Two of America's great judo champions—1996 Olympic bronze medalist and 1999 World Champion Jimmy Pedro (left) and seven-time U.S. lightweight National Champion Jimmy Martin—are shown walking off the mat together after a match.

LEFT-HANDERS   3.25

Left-handers have an advantage because there aren't that many of them. Consequently, left-handers get to work out with a lot of right-handers, while right-handers practice with very few left-handers. The result is that right-handers have a more difficult time with left-handers since they build up less resistance to left-handed attacks.

Right-handers would be wise to practice left-handed techniques. Former U.S. Olympian Jim Wooley used to hold a right hand and execute a left-hand *sodetsurikomi goshi* (hanging-sleeve shoulder throw), and it caught a lot of people off-guard. Toshihiko Koga of Japan (1989 and 1991 World Champion, and 1992 Olympic Champion) executes both right- and left-handed *ippon seoinage* (one-armed shoulder throw). Keven Asano, the U.S. silver medalist in the 1988 Olympics, executes both right- and left-handed techniques. Jimmy Pedro, 1999 world champion, attacks from any angle, with any technique, from any side.

Executing a left-handed technique—if you are a right-hander—feels uncomfortable in the beginning. However, you will eventually be able to execute the technique if you diligently work at it. It's just a matter of training your body to respond in a new way. If you execute a technique enough times, the synapses in your brain and body fire and form a pattern that will accommodate success. Do the novel. Do the unexpected. Increase your chances. Do it left!

The only problem a left-hander has is meeting another left-hander.

Whether it's Pop Warner football or Little League base-ball, parents will be parents. It's no different in any other sport, including judo. Parents want their kids to succeed and be able to do the things they were unable to do in their own youth. To accomplish this goal, some parents will go to extremes.

One of the biggest problems occurs in sports with weight divisions, such as judo. Time and again, parents will have their kids cut weight to make a lower division. The idea is not so bad with adults who have reached their growth potential, but for kids it is a case of poor judgment for the following reasons:

1. Kids are asked or told to cut weight when they are in a growth period. This is an important time when the body should not be deprived of any nutrients necessary for growth.

2. The underlying message sent to the child is "win at all costs." Forget the long-term effects and go for the short-term gain. And we wonder why young adults use anabolic steroids or drugs.

3. At its worst, kids will say "Oh, it's OK to have a win-at-all-costs attitude when it's your idea, but if I have it, it's not OK."

4. Kids who weigh 100 pounds or less who have to cut five or six pounds have a much more difficult time of it than adults who weigh 140 pounds or more who need to cut five or six pounds.

Kids should enjoy judo and take advantage of its positive qualities. Judo training should be a time of play and personal development. Cutting weight would do more harm than good.

Two-time judo grand champion George Harris shows us what training kids is all about. He lets them have fun while trying to find their own confidence level.

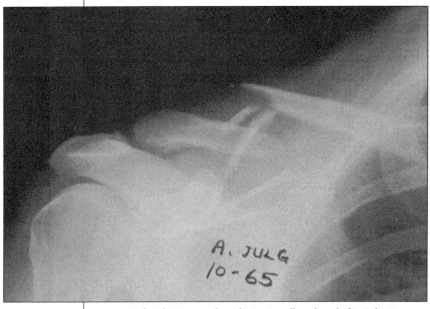

A clavicle injury such as this is virtually unheard of in judo. A person usually knows when his injury is serious, but it's always prudent to check with a physician.

SOME ADVICE FOR PHYSICAL AILMENTS   3.27

Physical ailments are just that: physical. Once in a while, some competitors use them as a crutch or a cross. A crutch is the excuse given for a poor performance. There is always an injury to blame. A cross is that, despite my injury, I continue. I'm tough. This becomes a mental game. You should stop and ask yourself, "Am I really hurt?" If you answer, "Yes," then stop. If you answer, "No," then keep going.

If you blame poor performance on an injury, you probably won't get to the root of the problem. Your poor performance can be the result of several factors, rather than just your injury. You will determine these factors more slowly if you create a psychological ailment as an added impediment to success.

Immediately ice your injuries. It causes vessel constriction and keeps the swelling down. Ice should be the order for one to 24 hours after an injury, depending on its severity.

If the injury is serious, you should consult your doctor. Have your physician examine knee injuries in particular, especially if you heard a snapping sound when the injury occurred.

Most minor sprains and strains heal within six to eight weeks. During the latter weeks of recovery, it may be advisable that you train in a manner that doesn't exacerbate the injury.

Judoka rely more and more now on video replays of their performance for the following reasons:

1. To scout the opponent to see what techniques he is using and what weaknesses he might have.
   If you really study a videotape of an opponent, you can see attack patterns and cues, such as certain grips or stances, that the opponent gives off just as he is about to enter into a technique. If you know what these cues are, you will be much better prepared. Pertaining to his weaknesses, wouldn't it be better to know that he lost his last five matches in *newaza?* Then prepare to do newaza.

2. To study and learn techniques and strategies.
   There are a number of videos that teach you how to execute certain techniques. These videos will help you understand the mechanics of the throw. Some moves are new. If you study them you will learn not only new techniques but also how to defend against them.

3. To study oneself in competition and analyze strengths and weaknesses.
   Many times when we view ourselves on video we study our opponent instead of our own performance. Also, we spend more time amusing ourselves than critically analyzing what we should or should not be doing. Here's your chance now. Videotape away—but don't forget to analyze your own performance.

4. For inspiration.
   There are a few inspirational videos on judo. For the most part, however, videos are boring if they are poorly prepared and recommended viewing if

professionally prepared. You must glean the inspirational parts of a video. They're there, waiting for your inspiration.

5. For recreation.
   Even if you don't study judo videos, you can still enjoy them. Usually, these videos are professionally prepared and contain footage shot at notable events such as tournaments. You will learn from watching them. Anyone not relying on videos is at a definite disadvantage. Videos are valuable tools from which you can study your performance in the *dojo* or at a tournament, or learn new techniques.

When you're busy working out, you can't tell whether what you're doing is right or wrong. By videotaping your workouts, you can study your performance and can determine the necessary adjustments to make.

Photo by Christine Penick Lincoln

Brian and Christoph Leininger (center), both former National Champions, are shown warming up at the Olympic Training Center in Colorado Springs, Colorado, after a short three-or-four-day tapering period.

TAPERING

Most *judoka* work out almost to the day before a competition, hoping to get that last ounce of edge that will defeat their opponents. In fact, their workouts also intensify as if to tempt fate. If you must work out, it's best to limit the workouts to pre-patterned attacks and light *randori* (free sparring).

Your peak performance and peak workouts should be at their highest level somewhere between the third and second week before a major competition. The intensity level should diminish from the third week prior to your match.

What does this do for you? Well, for one it allows time for minor injuries to heal. And most importantly, it greatly reduces your injury rate. Most accidents tend to happen when your stress level is high, such as right before a competition. Also, you can store glycogen during this period. And should you suffer an injury while tapering, it would most likely be minor and would still enable you to fight.

CHAPTER
OUTCOME
4

"KEKKA"

結果

Anyone could become conceited or egotistical, or have delusions of grandeur. No matter how good anyone becomes, somewhere, somehow, someone can defeat what Father Time has yet to take away. Someone tougher than you is always out there somewhere. He may not be in your sport, but he's out there.

"Egotism is the anesthetic that kills the pain of stupidity."
—Knute Rockne

As World and Olympic champion Katsuhiko Kashiwazaki; said, "When you win a world title you are a champion for that day. The next day you could lose to the same person you beat the day before. When you're a champion you can look down and there are a lot of people below you. When you look up there's always someone above you."

Photo by Hayward Nishioka

When you look up, there's always someone above you.
When you look down, there's always someone below you.

From L to R: Randy Harrelle, Kenny Patteson and Christophe Leininger

Below from L to R: Pete Christiansen, Faith Urban, Hayward Nishioka, Susan Kim and Richard Lewis

Above from L to R: Mohsen Jamal, Merdad Aflaki and Neil Urban

From L to R: Gerald Diggs, Hayward Nishioka and Nick Rivera.

These are but a few people who have contributed to the growth of judo.

Photos courtesy of Hayward Nishioka and Richard Lewis

SMALL JUDO, BIG JUDO   4.2

Small judo is involved with judo techniques and skills. Big judo is concerned with the elevation of life. It means taking the lessons we learn while practicing judo and applying their principles to improve our everyday lives.

Judo training affords us opportunities to be courageous, honest, economic, creative, respectful, insightful, thoughtful, healthy and confident. All of these attributes make us more productive citizens, which is more important than just being a champion. That's big judo.

"What athletics teaches is the self-discipline of hard work and sacrifice necessary to achieve a goal. Nowadays, too many people are looking for a shortcut. Life is the same as athletics. You have to work to accomplish anything." Roger Staubach former NFL Quarterback -Dallas Cowboys

Older Japanese *sensei* often say of a competitor *"Anoshito wa ningen ga dekiteiru,"* which means, "That person has reached a level where his humanity is developed to a sufficient level." Now, a value other than being a champion suddenly enters the picture. But wait. Don't we think of champions as heroes, made of the "right stuff" and representing all that is good? This raises the question of whether moralistic attributes should be attached to what is essentially a physical sport.

The founder of judo seemed to think so. Dr. Jigoro Kano, who was acquainted with the two famous American educators John Dewey and Jessie Ferrings Williams, believed—as they did—that valuable lessons could be learned through engaging in physical activity. From the onset of training we are aware that judo is an inherently dangerous sport. There are techniques in the judo arsenal that can maim and even kill someone. Although we would never go that far and have safeguards that prevent us from going that far, we need to pay thoughtful attention to this type of power. Indeed, along with this power comes a duty to use it reasonably and for the betterment of mankind. For now you have the power of life and death—to injure or not to injure—in the palms of your hands and the soles of your feet.

Other values are gleaned from the practice of judo, such as bravery—that you fight your match even though you're so nervous that you feel sick and want to scrap the whole endeavor; skill—that you have learned techniques to help you attain your goal more easily; advancement—that if you keep trying, things will get better; and cooperation—that through working with others you can improve and create something that couid not have been created if you worked alone. Dr. Kano formulated three precepts or maxims that summarized what judo was for. They are:

jiko no kansei—self-perfection

jitta kyoe—mutual welfare and benefit

seiryoku zenryo—maximum efficiency with minimum effort

There are experiences in the physical world that translate into our everyday lives and subtly change us forever. The thing that haunts me, though, is the question "When do we know?" At what level can we say to ourselves "anoshi-to wa ningen ga dekiteiru"?

Anton Geesink (standing, right), World and Olympic judo champion and member of the International Olympic Committee, helping to build character in the youth of today, the citizens of tomorrow.

Takahiko Ishikawa is one of Japan's most famous *judoka*. Once, while training in Puerto Rico, he was gentle with the people he was training with, and they mistook it for weakness. Ishikawa went into high gear at the next training session. As a result, his training companions did a lot of grunting and groaning, and suffered from headaches. Ishikawa later humbled himself and apologized for being rough. Now his training companions knew what humility meant.

WORTH

Of course, champions are cocky sometimes. They must feel and know that they can surmount any obstacle and that they're better than others.

Nevertheless, it's always nice to see someone go beyond being just a throwing and pinning machine and display humility, intelligence and humanness. The question is, would you still be a person whom others would regard highly if you weren't a judo champion?

The priest Takuan Osho once asked of Miyamoto Musashi, "What would you be without a sword?"

That is the question I always pose to those seeking to enter into the sport of judo.

If the answer is yes then teaching judo is easy. If the answer is anything else, it's a challenge. Judo is difficult because by it's very nature it's tough on the body and tough to acclimate yourself to. Right away there are all these foreign words and customs to get used to. It's hard to remember when to sit, when to stand, when to bow and to whom, and with what feeling. Oh, and the teacher: No "sensei" gets upset because the belt isn't tied on right.

And what's this? I have to bow to a person who's going to try to beat the living snot out of me? What about all these techniques that are to be learned; do I really need to learn them all? It takes a long time to learn even one throw. It takes time to memorize Japanese judo terms. There are 65 throws in the "Gokyono Waza" alone, and that's not counting mat work, falling or unorthodox techniques.

Also that "Randori" session—now that's a killer. That's where you find yourself trying to find an opening to enter into a technique but can't. You're too busy trying to avoid being tossed as you stiffen every muscle in your body. In the meantime your muscle glycogen has depleted, lactic acid levels have tripled, your lungs are burning and your heart is about to pop. For the next few days you wake up to lactic-acid aftermath, where your muscles are crying out to you, "What the hell is going on?" If you're tough, you'll think about how to improve your performance. If not, it's going to be a challenge.

Judo is like putting together a jigsaw puzzle in which you've lost the box-cover picture to guide you. If you're committed, you just jump in and do it; over time you begin to fit the pieces together and a pattern emerges. The more pieces that fit into place, the more defined the picture. As your defenses improve you will have a more economic use of your energy system and draw more from your aerobic system. Over time your conditioning will improve, allowing you more energy to enter into techniques. The more you enter into techniques, the better your skill level will become. The better your skill level gets, the more you will be throwing, pinning, choking, armbar executing and feeling those endorphins. In the end you will begin to understand what Jigoro Kano meant when he said "maximum efficiency with minimum effort."

But first, "Are you tough?"

Photo by Hayward Nishioka

In this competition let go, let God, and let a *tomoe nage* gain an *ippon.* Pan American Sports Director Frank Fullerton looks on as a lateral referee.

With a simple sweep of the feet at the right time and place, you've sealed your fate.

IT'S FATE? 4.6

Sometimes everything seems to be going right. Your practices have been great. You've been throwing everyone in sight. You've gotten a great draw, and all the other tough guys are in the other pool. Your first match is with a wimp. You go out, fight and lose. Even monkeys fall out of trees.

On another day, everything goes wrong. Everyone's been throwing and pinning you. Your sweetheart has left you for someone you thought was a nerd. Your first opponent looks like Baby Huey, and your second looks like The Terminator. You go out, fight and win. Does it make any sense? It's fate?

A couple of old-timers were talking after judo practice. "Judo was better in the old days. At least everyone had their basics down."

The other gentleman lifts his shoulders slightly, takes in a breath and replies, "Shikata ga nai." Which means, "It can't be helped" or "There's no solution." The statement rhetoric and moot does beg the question of comparison. Are we speaking about techniques, etiquette, strength, character, or overall judo ability? Could it be that old-timers in reflection over past events tend only to call up the best of their past, leaving the perfunctory entry drills and mundane randori practices behind? Could it be that like the old-timers we too will someday recall those frozen memories that we have selected to remain and say, "Judo was better in the old days"?

A black-belt acquaintance of mine returning to judo with his grandkids after a hiatus of nearly 40 years remarked, "Wow, I hardly recognize judo. Blue gi's, no kohaku,(winner stay-up tournaments), no senseis sitting stoically at the head tables. Now you see angry coaches yelling from the sidelines, no sitting cross-legged through long speeches in Japanese, and you see more non-Asians than Asians. Plus, what's all these kokos and yukis? And what's up with the lack of ettiquet? I think things were better in the 1960s."

Much of what judo is today and may become in the future is partially dependent upon sociologic demand that are placed on judo. In 1882 the founder of judo started out with only nine students. By 1889 there were 1,500. By 1896 there were 8,375; there were 15,926 students in 1916; and 78,874 in 1936. Today there are more than 180 member nations, with France having 500,000 members, alone.

With an increase in numbers comes an increase in possibilities and patterns of development. The founder of judo, Dr. Jigaro Kano went from a small dojo to a bona fide system in four years when in 1886 his style defeated all others in a police-sponsored tournament. By 1903, judo was internationalized with the teaching of Theodore Roosevelt, who was eventually awarded a brown belt.

With Gunji Koizumi and Mikinosuke Kawaishi in Europe, judo began to spread and in 1936 the first European Championships were held, and the sport of judo was born. In 1956 (after World War II) the first Worlds Championships were held. Judo was first included in the Olympics in 1964.

Since its inclusion into the Olympic family, the competition has been keen. What used to be somewhat of a game of chance is now a very calculated process. Countries that win on a consistent basis follow certain patterns of trainings. To be in the ballpark. Their contestants still practice randori , but in addition do much of the following: aerobic training, strength training, study videotapes and their performance, train for specific contestants, study tactics, study bio-mechanics and be psychologically tested. They study the rules and even the referee; The rules and the referees dictate the way judo is contested.

That's why judo looks the way it does. "Shikata ga nai."

Photo by Hayward Nishioka

Sometimes negative things happen. Our goal is to prepare ourselves so that we lessen the times we may say *"Shikata ga nai"* and in its stead say *"Shikata ga aru."* It *can* be helped.

Djamel Bouras turns Toshihiko Koga's body and world upside down. Koga was a shoo-in to win this match. He surely will replay this loss in his mind for years to come. Bouras gold, Koga silver. 1996 Olympic Games, Atlanta, GA.

AFTER THE FACT, WALTER MITTY   4.8

Have you ever suffered a loss or an indignity, then suddenly opened the drawer titled "mental playbacks"?

Usually, you go back in time mentally and reverse the situation. You picture in your mind what you should have done. Sometimes, if you were verbally assaulted, you think of a clever comeback. It's sad to say, but the "time of heaven" has passed by then. The moment when you should have retorted has slipped away. Nevertheless, this practice is good because it irks you and prods you to prepare for the next time. It is really not all that bad being Walter Mitty. Unlike poor Walter, however, our plight is closer to fulfillment since most of us put thoughts into action and gain results.

God, I'm tired of answering the question, "Who will win the confrontation between a *judoka* and a *karateka?*" So I won't.

What intrigues me more is the question, "What is the best combination and percentage of factors that would give me the greatest probability of winning? The choices are strength, skill, cardiovascular endurance, flexibility, agility, speed, experience and coordination."

Here's the Russian model: Strength, endurance, and skill of a different sort. The Japanese model consists of skill first and foremost, then endurance. It's the tiger and the lion in battle. Who will win? Which combination is better?

Photo by Christine Penick Lincoln

Dan Hatano (left) and Todd Brehe (right) are fighting it out to see who will win.

The person in the white judo *gi* is lifting his opponent over with his leg as the person in the blue gi demonstrates his ability to twist out of the throw by using his head as a focal point.

"Nebari" means "viscous or sticky." *"Zuoi"* or *"tsuoi"* means "strong." In combination, the word *"nebarizuoi"* means "tenacious" or "persevering," which is a quality necessary for success in judo. Even though you are pulled or pushed around, or twisted or knocked down, you don't give up and you somehow wriggle out of adverse situations. You attack no matter what you are up against.

Nicolas Gil of Canada came from behind twice. The first time he did so, his opponent was Ben Spijkers of Holland. During the match, Spijkers was ahead by a half-point. Gil kept attacking, but he could score only a *yuko* (superior advantage) against the Dutchman. Then, with less than 10 seconds left in the match, Gil unleashed a *haraigoshi* that gained him a half-point. At the bell, Spijkers had a half-point and Gil had a half-point plus the earlier yuko. Gil was the winner.

The second time Gil came from behind, his opponent was 1991 World Champion Hidetaka Okada of Japan. Everyone who witnessed this match seemed to have that "Oh well" look on his face. Okada scored first with a yuko and a *tomoenage* (stomach throw). Gil kept fighting and attacking, but it was to no avail. With less than 40 seconds to go in the match, Gil took advantage of Okada's off-balanced body position and knocked him down for a *wazari*. Okada, realizing there was not enough time left in the match to catch up, gave up.

Gil, on the other hand, never gives up. Anyone aspiring to succeed in judo has to be able to withstand setbacks and losses and continue to fight. For example, Daruma dolls, with their weighted round bottoms, continue to return to an upright position even though they are knocked about. That's what is needed in judo as well as in life. Now, that's nebarizuoi.

Isn't it a curiosity that upon returning from a respite you seem better than when you left? You are suddenly able to throw people you were unable to throw before. Why?

And why is it that three or four days later, you are not able to do as well? Perhaps when you returned you were enthusiastic once again. What made you enthusiastic, and how can you maintain this enthusiasm? This is indeed an interesting phenomenon which, if studied, may yield some positive results.

Photo by Hayward Nishioka

Freshness, intensity and focus are but a few of the qualities necessary for judo success.

Like a recurring theme, 1991 World Champion David Khakhaleshvili
of Georgia wins the 1996 European Championship again over Imre
Csosz of Hungary.

DÉJÀ VU

I've been in this situation before! I know what's going to happen next. God, this is weird. It's like an instant replay. But will you win or lose? Can you change what you know has already been set in stone? Will you change the course of your history in time? Now the feeling fades, the vision subsides, the moment no longer has meaning. But will it happen again? Will you be able to alter what you perceive as fate? Yes!

"One day, as if by magic I was fairly strong. I was no longer robotic in my movements and throws. I was no longer being tossed and turned at every step. I was now in command. I was now the one throwing. It felt great!"—Merdad Aflaki.

It's funny, but it's the same in almost every endeavor. You start out rigid and unskilled, and with time you improve. Improvement seems slow as you wonder if you'll ever get good. Imperceptive to your own eyes and senses, you creep along until one day someone says, "Hey, you're pretty tough now." Or, "Man, are you getting strong!" Or "Damn, you're good. I didn't think you would be able to throw me so easily."

Getting to this stage takes time and desire. Your successes will come slowly and periodically at first. You will experience surges of success now and then, until finally you'll arrive at the *dojo* for yet another practice session and—wham!—things will begin to click for you. Something has triggered your soul's success button. Don't expect it to happen until you've had a couple of hundred practice sessions with at least ten or more bouts of *randori* each session under your belt.

Make it so!

"Chiri mo tsumori yamato nari."—Even specks of dust when collected can form a mountain.

Isao Okano (right) skies his opponent at the All-Japan Championships.

Photo by Christine Penick Lincoln

Tournament competitors are getting ready to compete, and they are giving each other advice.

TAKING CRITICISM

Sensei: "Joe, you've got to do more large major throws like *seoinage, haraigoshi or uchimata.*"

Parent: "Joe, you've got to do more *ashiwaza,* like *okuri-ashibarai* (chasing foot sweep) or *kouchigari.*"

Friend: "Joe, forget the standing techniques. Your strong point is on the mat."

Sit down, stand up, go left, go right, get lower, get stronger, loosen up, bend your knees, pull harder, push more ... Damn! Who do I listen to?

Beep! Beep! Beep! Mental overload, conflicting information. Shut-down time. Grrrr ...

Take what works, and store the rest. When you become successful, they'll ask *you* for advice.

After a while, *judoka* learn to use their energy wisely. Instead of going all-out for as long as they can go, they learn to distribute their energy. It's fun to work with beginners who don't yet understand this principle, and let them fire away at you with all their strength and energy. Then, after they have depleted all the glycogen stored in their muscles, they begin to huff and puff. They begin to tire physically, and thus become affected psychologically. In their minds, they're softly saying "Whew! I'm tired! Damn, I don't know if I can keep up. Damn, I can't go on. I give up. Hell, let them throw me. Who cares?!" Wham! Gotcha! As one great football coach once remarked, "Fatigue makes cowards of us all."

It's like in the old Westerns, when the bad guy uses six bullets and the good guy on the white horse says "You've used up your six. I got five left!" The bad guy's only response is to gulp or use some other appropriate four-letter word.

It's also like when someone's red-hot mad at you. You let him talk on and on, and when he's finished, you ask "Is there anything else? What else?"

Photo © Bob Willingham, 1998

When you're tired and spent you're more likely to make mistakes, such as the one made by the competitor in the white *gi*. His mistake sent his opponent flying.

Photo by Christine Penick Lincoln

Dan Hatano's (top) opponent is wearing a double-weave *gi*.

MAGIC JUDO *GI* 4.16

For manufacturers like Dan-Rho, Mizuno and Adidas, *gi* sales have been magical. Are gi really worth $125 to $250 each? Some gi companies seem to think so, because that's how much they charge for them. On the other hand, you can buy single-weave gi for $30 to $40 each. Does it make a difference? Yes. How much of a difference? Oh, about a hundred dollars or so.

A double-weave gi lasts longer; and besides, if it feels good on you, you usually perform better. At least you know if you don't perform as well it's not because you lack a good gi.

When it comes down to it, your gi doesn't do your judo for you. That's why manufacturers pay champions to don their brand name so the brand name is associated with the champion. People buy the brand name and vicariously become the champion. It's good for business. But maybe, just maybe, it might be the thing that helps you psychologically. If it is, your gi may just be magical.

Now, can I sell you a magic carpet?

After all the learning and practicing that we do, after all the times we compete against and fight with each other, we are still *judoka*. There is something about this sport akin to a fraternity or sorority. Once you reach a certain level, in most cases black belt, you're one of the boys (or girls). You're never alone! You can go to virtually any state in the union, or even to another country for that matter, find a *dojo*, train with the students there, and go for a brew and compare war stories.

Even those who no longer get out on the mat and mix it up anymore belong to this "fraternity" if they've put in their time. Each judoka in the fraternity wordlessly and almost inherently knows he shares a common bond that is difficult to attain; a bond formed by years of contracting muscles, effort, sweat and tears, fulfilled and unfulfilled dreams, aches and pains and the occasional visit to the victory stand. From the aspirant to the Olympic champion to the old *sensei*, we share a grand title: We are judoka.

Pictured in this photo, which was taken in 1932, are all the original
10th *dans* in judo except one.

Photo by Hayward Nishioka

Pictured are 30-years-and-over-masters-division players having fun. Many are *sensei*, referees or helpers, but at the *dojo* they are "giving back" to a sport that means a lot to them.

TURNING POINT   4.18

A visit by Father Time occurs to the most seemingly invincible *judoka*. Only after a while, this visitor becomes a permanent resident. Knock, knock, it's Father Time. Ah, bovine dung. I'll continue forever.

Oh, yeah? That's what *you* think. The nerves are the first to diminish, decreasing your reaction and movement time. Your muscles atrophy unnoticeably at first, then— bingo, bango—an injury prevents you from being able to work out. The chest you once had becomes an inflated tummy. Your flexibility goes, too. Strenuous workouts strain your heart and make your lungs burn.

Well, we all take our turn. Now it's time to give back. It's time to pass on your knowledge; hopefully, to push others beyond the point at which you ended your journey. Assist others as a referee, instructor, coach, trainer, administrator or supporter.

"Kimura no mae wa kimura nashi Kimura no ato wa Kimura nashi"

"Before Kimura there was no Kimura. After Kimura there is no Kimura."

He was never defeated in major competition.

Just say "No"!

ALL-TIME U.S. OLYMPIC JUDO MEDALISTS

on top of the world

DRUG FREE

Eddie Liddie

Mike Swain

Jason Morris

Bob Berland

Kevin Asano

Jim Bregman

Allen Coage

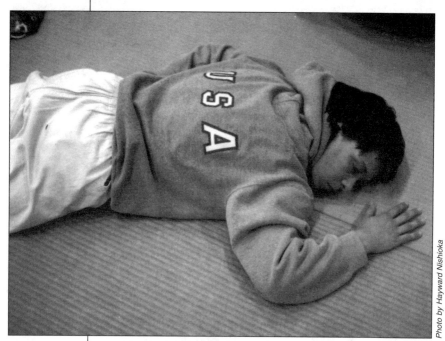

Dr. Ann Marie Rousey, our first world champion in judo, is shown here resting between special intensive work sessions. Those in judo know it takes time to excel. No doubt Dr. Rousey is winning other battles in dreamland.

JUDO: THE PHYSICS OF DRUG PREVENTION   4.20

In 1996 a friend of mine, who is a psychologist, spoke to me about this book while she was visiting me in Los Angeles. I was talking to her about the story "It's Who You Hang With." (see section 1.7) She remarked that she had a similar idea, which she referred to as "Judo: The Physics of Drug Prevention." I, being curious about that title, replied "OK, I'll bite. What do judo, physics and drugs have in common?"

Here's her answer: "Matter cannot occupy two spaces at the same time. If you're practicing judo, you're not out on the streets doing drugs." How simple, yet profound. We never stop to think of all the positive qualities we glean from our sport. All the long-lasting lessons, subtly passed on by quiet acts of courage displayed by those who give of themselves in this sport.

And who is this friend who spoke to me about judo and drug prevention? Dr. Ann Marie (Burns) Rousey. Those of us who practice judo remember her as Ann Marie Burns, the first person from the United States to win a world championship in judo.

It's bad. It's inevitable. It divides good fortune from misfortune. When we gain from it, it's good. When we are on the wrong end of the stick, it's bad. What is it? Judo politics.

Those who are adept or are inadvertently put into a politically advantageous position may gain from judo politics; those who are not will not. Fletcher Thornton, an international referee, once delicately remarked, "Sometimes decisions are made in judo that have nothing to do with one's ability in judo. It has to do with who you know." Then are judo politics really necessary?

Leon Garrie, former vice president and founder of California Judo Inc., spoke about the inevitability of politics. He said: "Politics are everywhere; we can't escape them. You're here because of the politics between your mother and father." Somewhere along the line, you will be affected—both negatively and positively—by politics. What is important is that you do your best so you know for yourself that you did not let yourself down or use politics as an excuse for inability.

Moreover, when or if you eventually find yourself in a position of power, it is important that you remember political inequities and make the fairest decisions for your fellow *judoka*. It is also important that you not act condescending or haughty toward those who are not politically astute or are not of your persuasion.

I am reminded of what Okakura Tenshin said in *The Book of Tea* about the overestimation of our value system and the neglect of what we think are lesser people: "Those who cannot feel the littleness of great things in themselves are apt to overlook the greatness of little things in others."

Photo by Hayward Nishioka

Pictured here are attendees at the very first meeting of California Judo Inc., which was held at Los Angeles City College in 1980. Third from left is Leon Garrie, the organization's architect. Hayward Nishioka, the organization's first president, is taking the picture.

Photo by Philip Porter

10th degree black belt Charles Palmer, the referee standing at right, is a pioneer leader of modern judo rules. He was also the president of the International Judo Federation during the 1960s.

REFEREES I HAVE KNOWN

It's the referee's fault that I lost. If I had a better referee, I would have won. I got screwed again!

It's a common complaint that the referee was at fault. However, did you ever think that for every time you lost a match due to a referee, you also won a match due to a referee? If in a year's worth of matches you received fifty percent of the bad calls in your favor, that may not be too bad.

Granted, there are tough opponents who can be defeated by only a *koka* or a *kinsa,* but how about some ability? If you just go out there and smash your opponent, how can you go wrong? "Still, it seems I've gotten more rotten calls than good ones," you may say. Might it be a personality problem? Naaaah!

Remember the referee's lament: "When I do something right, no one remembers. When I do something wrong, no one forgets!" Ask any referee how much he gets paid for doing this job. Ask him how much of his own money he has spent to travel to events in order to referee. Ask him how many people critique him. Ask him why he referees. Now ask yourself, "Can I referee?"

Why are there coaches? Why aren't there competitor/coaches? I'm not sure. There probably are some people that can do both. But let's think about this. How good are you at yelling at and intimidating referees and officials? Ooops, damn, the official refereeing my match is the same guy I yelled at during Joe's match. Now I have to fight Joe, my own teammate. I've coached him really well; plus, he's stronger than me. Oh well, if he beats me I'm still a good coach. But what if I win? Does it mean I'm a bad coach or a good player, or just a guy with a conflict of interest?

Do I have time as a coach to study all my team members' opponents? Will I have time to adjust to the players' idio-syncrasies and coach them accordingly? Have I studied game plans, diets, sleep habits, practice rhythms, tech-niques, conditioning and psyches?

Coaches are a special breed. The original word "coach," I'm told, came from the idea of riding coaches that trans-ported people from one place to another. Like these coaches, we are to take a competitor from one place to another: from beginner to advanced, non-champion to champion, boy to man and bad to good.

Photo by Hayward Nishioka

Coaches have it rough. They see what can be done. They can yell encouragement to the competitor from beside the ring, but that's all. The person standing is Keith Nakasone.

Tsutomu Ohshima is seated in the front row, third from left. Hayward Nishioka is seated in the second row, far left. This photograph was taken in 1965.

IT'S PART OF THE PROCESS; YOU NEVER LOSE 4.24

When you lose a match, you gain an experience. Most competitors overlook this fact, since they think only of the results, and not the overall process, of the competition. One tournament is roughly worth ten practice sessions. Yes, you hate to lose. Yes, there is a chance you will bruise your ego. Yes, you may never win. Yes, you may cry. But yes, you will learn from it.

If you're afraid to put yourself on the line and are constantly worried about losing, it's probably time to begin training in another sport. I can't think of a judo champion who has never lost a match. I can't think of a black belt who was never a white belt. I can't think of a 20-year-old who was never a one-year-old. I can't think of walking a mile without a first step, a fiftieth step, and a thousandth step. Each step is a building block, with its own tests and learning situations. Those who have "the right stuff" go on and learn from the experience. Don't be afraid to lose.

Tsutomu Ohshima once told his student about three types of people. The first was the idiot. He stepped into a manhole, came back day after day, and kept falling into the manhole. The second was the average man. He stepped into the manhole, crawled out, and was cautious of that manhole the next day. The third was the genius. He was the one across the street who watched all this and said to himself, "I'll just avoid that situation."

All of us at different times in our lives play out these roles. The trick is to be more than average. In judo, you—the average person—are trying to become a genius during a high-stress situation. If you're afraid to experience the unknown, you will never learn. Don't be afraid to take part in the learning process.

As a youth I had been in many an affray over my racial heritage. The term "Jap" was applied liberally as I bounced from one fight to another. This took its toll mentally as well as physically as I often wondered who and what I was. Americans from the United States considered me a Japanese. Japanese from Japan perceived me as an American.

This problem, which I thought of only in exclusive terms, is in reality shared by many people who are trying to make adjustments in our multi-culturally rich society. The answer to my own dilemma didn't come for some time and is still being digested over the years.

A love for judo and intense workout sessions in search of techniques eventually paid off as I earned a berth on a U.S. International judo team. I fought hard at the 1967 Pan-American Games, and as the day came to an end fate passed its golden wand over me and I took the decision and the gold medal in judo over Brazil's Luhfe Shiozawa. Funny, the thing I remember most about that victory was standing on the uppermost platform feeling the hair on the back of my head stand at attention as "The Star-Spangled Banner" was played. And from that moment on in my subconscious mind, I knew that whatever anyone might say or do, I was an American.

While this was an answer to my own existence, judo, like so many sports, provides many avenues to success. Each practice session is a search for excellence and self-worth. Its physicality builds strength, endurance and skills, in turn giving you confidence, courage, determination and a plan for success. It's a rite of passage.

These are all qualities that make a society great. They elevate the human spirit in a microcosm where overcoming the risk of failure elevates you to the status of hero but never villain.

This is the U.S. Goodwill Team, which traveled to Holland, Great Britain, France and Belgium in 1964. From left to right are: George Harris, Hayward Nishioka, Phil Porter, Tosh Seino, Kenneth Kuniyuki and Richard Fukuwa.

I am fortunate to have met many masters, among them Shigeru Egami *sensei* and Morihei Uyeshiba sensei during my lifetime. Both Egami and Uyeshiba were powerful beyond belief, but they possessed enigmatic qualities contrary to that of defeating another human being. Their gentleness, kindness and love were magnified and deepened by their opposite ability to control life and death.

Photo courtesy of Shigeru Egami

Shigeru Egami

I can picture Egami sensei smiling innocently as he sits in a swing at a playground. This was the photograph he chose for the front cover of his "special edition" book on karate—an odd choice for a person whom many people

Morihei Uyeshiba

feared, respected and loved. When I asked Uyeshiba sensei what to him was the most important lesson to be learned from practicing the martial arts, he smiled and replied, "Love." The way he smiled and said the word invoked a different meaning and experience than the way we define the word "love."

I feel fortunate that I was able to walk on earth at the same time Egami and Uyeshiba did. They were able to teach me so much because they had come full-circle in their training. I learned from them to be able to relax, and to be kind, considerate and caring of fellow human beings. I think they knew how to simplify life because they had found themselves. May your judo training develop such character.